Design

The design of the *Yamato* class battleships grew out of Japanese resentment at the outcome the 1921 Washington Naval Treaty and the 1930 London Naval Treaty. These negotiations, in which Great Britain accepted parity with the United States, forced Japan to agree to a 5:5:3 ratio in capital ships – three for every five in the Royal and US Navies. When Japan invaded Manchuria, China in 1934, the League of Nations imposed sanctions upon Japan, at which point Japan dropped out of the League and abandoned all naval treaties. Already inferior in numbers, the Imperial Japanese Navy planned to redress the balance with ships more powerful than those of its rivals and likely enemies, so the designs for a new class of battleship that began at this point were unrestricted by any of the previous treaty limitations.

During the years 1934 to 1937 about twenty-four different designs were drawn up. Displacements ranged from 49,000 to 69,000 tons, speeds from 24 to 31 knots, various forms of a combined steam and diesel power plant were considered, and main gun calibres from 16in to 18in. Twin, triple and even quad mounts were proposed for the main armament, in different arrangements, including a layout similar to that of the British battleship *Nelson*. By late 1935 a design requirement of nine 18in guns in three triple turrets and a top speed of at least 27 knots had been established. The use of diesel engines was dropped from consideration, as the Japanese Navy was having trouble with some of their larger diesel power plants, and the complexity and cost of removing and replacing them in a capital ship would be too high. By early 1937 the final design of this new class of battleship was completely steam powered. The final design was approved in March 1937, but the first vessel, *Yamato*, could not be laid down until improvements to the yard facilities could be completed. The navy yards were well set up to construct battleships, but not on the scale of these new behemoths. The construction facilities had to be widened, lengthened and the approaches dredged deeper.

The Japanese wanted to keep the construction of this new class of warship a total secret, so there was a complete restriction on photography, as well as the construction of a roof over part of the building slip; there was even a gigantic curtain of rope used to block any view of construction and at Nagasaki a 400-ton camouflage net. These efforts to keep information from the Americans were generally

Yamato running full power sea trials off Sata Point, Sukumo, on 30 October 1941.

Another view of *Yamato* at full power trials in relatively heavy weather in the Inland Sea, 16 October 1941.

successful, and by 1942, although the US Navy knew of the construction of at least two new battleships, they only had a rough sketch of the vessels. In fact, the US Navy's Office of Naval Intelligence assumed that these vessels were armed with 16in guns and displaced 45,000 tons, and did not know the size of the main guns and the actual displacement of the battleships until after the war.

After the extensive modification to the Kure, Nagasaki, Yokosuka and even the Sasebo naval shipyards, which also included heavy lift equipment for the construction of these massive warships, *Yamato*'s keel was laid down in the dry dock at the Kure Navy Yard on 4 November 1937.

Prior to this, extensive research was conducted in hull model tank testing to develop the most efficient hull form possible. It was found that the large bulbous bow reduced hull resistance by over 8 per cent, as well as increasing buoyancy forward in heavy seas. It was also discovered that careful streamlining of the propeller shafts and the bilge keel added at least half a knot at full speed. Because of this research *Yamato* was able to achieve her maximum speed of 27.5 knots and an efficient cruising speed of 16 to 18 knots with only 150,000shp on a vessel displacing over 70,000 tons. Because of the extreme

■ *YAMATO* CLASS BATTLESHIPS

Name	Builder	Laid Down	Launched	Completed
YAMATO	Kure Navy Yard	4 Nov 1937	8 Aug 1940	16 Dec 1941
MUSASHI	Mitsubishi, Nagasaki	29 Mar 1938	1 Nov 1940	5 Aug 1942
SHINANO	Yokosuka Navy Yard	4 May 1940	Converted to aircraft carrier	
No 111	Kure Navy Yard	7 Nov 1940	Broken up on slip 1942	

DESIGN CHARACTERISTICS (1942)

Dimensions	Length, oa 863ft; wl 840ft; Beam, oa 121ft; Draught, 35ft 7in
Displacement	64,000 tons standard load; 67,123 tons trial load; 69,988 tons full load.
Armament	Nine (3x3) 18.1in; twelve (4x3) 6.1in; twelve (6x2) 5in DP; twenty-four (8x3) 25mm AA; four (2x2) 13mm AA
Protection	Belt 16.1in; Bulkheads 11.8in; Deck 7.9 to 9.1in; Barbettes 21.5in; Conning Tower 19.7in; Main Turrets – Face 24.8in, Sides 9in, Roof 10 in
Machinery	Twelve Kampon boilers; four-shaft Kampon geared turbines
Bunkerage	6300 tons fuel oil
Performance	150,000 shaft horsepower; top speed 27.5 knots
Range	7200nm @ 16 knots
Aircraft	Three Aichi E13A1 'Jake' floatplanes
	Four Mitsubishi F1M2 'Pete' floatplanes
Catapults	Two Kure Type 2, Model 5
Complement	Officers 150; enlisted men 2150

breadth of the hull, *Yamato*'s draught was only four feet more than other battleships in the Japanese Navy that displaced 30,000 to 40,000 tons less.

Other innovations incorporated in the construction of these warships included the methods of hull plating, using a mixture of lap- and butt-jointed plates. The smoother butt-jointed plating was used fore and aft to reduce frictional resistance in those higher water pressure areas, while the stronger lap-jointed method was used over the central portion of the hull. Extensive use of electric welding, new to shipbuilding at that time, was also made, although more of this assembly technique was used in the construction of the superstructure than in the hull.

Another innovation in the construction of the *Yamato* was the use of the armour plating as part of the actual hull structure, as opposed to an add-on. This made the armour an integral part of the hull, thereby increasing the strength of the hull as well as reducing the weight of its construction. The weight of *Yamato*'s armour was the heaviest of any warship ever built, and the ship was divided into the most watertight compartments (1147) of any battleship in history. These features made this class by far the most difficult battleships to sink by bombs and/or torpedoes.

The *Musashi*'s keel was laid down on the slipway at the Mitsubishi Industries Dock Yard in Nagasaki on 29 March 1938. Later, from May to November of 1939, the boilers, reduction gear and steam turbines were installed into the hull of *Yamato*. Although the *Musashi* was laid down five months later than *Yamato*, her construction was progressing at a faster rate, so that *Musashi*'s propulsion machinery was installed at approximately the same time as *Yamato*'s.

In July of 1939 the Mitsubishi Dock Yard also began the construction of a 10,000-ton freighter, the *Kashino*, which was purpose-built for transporting the massive 18.1in main gun barrels and the associated turrets. These were constructed at the Kure Arsenal and had to be transported by this ship to Nagasaki for installation aboard *Musashi*. For this role the hull form was unique and unusually broad for a freighter of this size, in order to accommodate the huge barbette and main gun turret assemblies. *Kashino* was completed in July 1940, after a couple of grounding accidents during her trials delayed her commissioning. This in turn delayed the construc-

The anti-aircraft mounts aboard the *Musashi*, taken on 24 June 1943, when the Emperor Hirohito was visiting the ship. In this image the enclosed twin 5in and triple 25mm mounts, as well as the massive 150cm searchlights, can be seen. These last were director-controlled, in line with the high priority the IJN gave to night fighting, although the number was reduced later in the war and the positions used for AA directors.

Opposite, top: This is one of the very few surviving on-board photographs of the two *Yamato* class battleships. This was taken aboard the *Musashi* in June or July of 1942, while the ship was undergoing her trials, prior to her commissioning into the Imperial Japanese Navy.

Opposite, bottom: This image is a collage of two photographs taken aboard the *Musashi* in June or July 1942. It is a view looking down and aft from the machine gun control platform, which was on the seventh level of the bridge tower. The photographer was standing on the starboard platform for the twin 13mm machine guns.

Below: Admiral Yamamoto (front row, sixth from left) and his staff aboard the *Yamato* early in 1942, lined up behind the rear of the portside triple 6.1in turret. Note the complex shapes, and in particular the amount of curved steel surfaces, used in the construction of the superstructure.

■ FLOATPLANE CHARACTERISTICS

	Mitubishi F1M2 Type 0	Aichi E13A1 Type 0
Function	Two-seat short range observation	Three-seat long range reconnaissance
Floats	Single	Twin
Allied code name	Pete	Jake
Powerplant	Mitsubishji Zuisei 14cyl radial	Mitsubishi Kinsei 43 14cyl radial
Power	875hp max	1080hp
Wingspan	11m (36ft 1in)	14.5m (47ft 7in)
Length	9.5m (31ft 2in)	11.3m (37ft 1in)
Height	4m (13ft 1in)	7.4m (24ft 3in)
Weight loaded	2550kg (5622lb)	3640kg (8025lb)
Maximum speed	230mph @ 11,285ft	234mph @ 7155ft
Climb	9 min 30 sec to 5000m (16,405ft)	6 min 5 sec to 3000m (9845ft)
Ceiling	9440m (30,970ft)	8730m (28,640ft)
Range	400 nautical miles	1128 nautical miles
Guns, fixed	2 – 7.7mm Type 97 machine gun	–
Guns, swivelling, in rear cockpit	1 – 7.7mm Type 92 machine gun	1 – 7.7mm Type 92 machine gun
External stores	Two 60kg (132lb) bombs	Four 60kg (132lb) bombs or depth charges; or one 250kg (550lb) bomb

tion of the *Musashi* by at least two months. The freighter was then used to transport further mountings to Yokosuka for the third *Yamato* class battleship.

The keel of this ship was laid down on 4 May 1940 in the dry dock at the Yokosuka Navy Yard. At this time the third member of the *Yamato* class was not yet named and was known simply as 'Warship No 110'. She was to be built to a design slightly modified from that of the *Yamato* and *Musashi*, with slightly thinner armour, designed to withstand hits from 16in shells, as opposed to 18in shell protection of her sister-ships. Her beam was three feet narrower in an effort to increase her speed and she was to be fitted with the then new 3.9in twin mount AA weapon, as opposed to the 5in twin AA mounts fitted on the *Yamato* and *Musashi*.

In an effort to preserve the secrecy surrounding these warships, the mighty *Yamato* was 'launched' with little fanfare (actually floated out of the dry dock at the Kure Navy Yard) on 8 August 1940. Construction of her superstructure began at this point, as did the laying of her wooden decks. For these decks Japanese 'Hinoki' cypress was used, a relatively new timber first fitted to the Imperial Japanese Navy flagship *Nagato*. This wood was laid in smaller 5in widths, compared with the customary 7in wide teak planking fitted on all previous Japanese battleships.

The forecastle of the *Musashi* in July 1942. The crew paraded on deck give a very clear idea of the massive proportions of the ship.

The *Musashi* was launched on 1 November 1940, setting a record weight for a conventional slipway of 35,737 tons. The fourth and final *Yamato* class battleship had its keel laid down on 7 November 1940 in the same dry dock in which the *Yamato* had been built at the Kure Navy Yard. At that time this vessel was known as 'Warship No 111', and was to be a duplicate of No 110, a modified *Yamato* class.

Work was progressing at a steady rate on both the *Yamato* and the *Musashi* throughout early 1941. The gigantic size of these two warships was becoming apparent as the superstructures took form. The construction of the main gun turrets had actually started as far back as early 1940, but their complexity meant that they were not ready much before the point of completion of the entire vessel. *Yamato* had her main gun barrels installed during the months of May to July 1941.

In early October 1941 the *Kashino* transported the first of the massive 18.1in gun barrels for the second of the class, and thereafter would make regular trips from the Kure Naval Ordnance Arsenal to the Mitsubishi Industries Dock Yard to transport the turret components and the rest of the main gun barrels for the *Musashi*.

By late October, *Yamato* was running her trials in the Inland Sea, which went on into November. Numerous short voyages out to the Inland Sea were needed to calibrate and work up all equipment, including weapons, machinery, rangefinders, and many other aspects of this completely new weapons platform. Her final fitting out and adjustments after trials continued into December 1941.

■ SHIP'S BOATS

Type	Length	Propulsion	Number
Pinnace	17m (55ft 9in)	150hp steam	Two
Barge	15m (49ft 3in)	150hp motor	One
Launch	12m (39ft 4in)	30hp motor	Four
Motor boat	11m (36ft 0in)	60hp motor	One
Motor dory	8m (26ft 3in)	10hp motor	One
Cutter	9m (29ft 6in)	Rowed/sailed	Four
Dinghy	6m (19ft 8in)	Rowed/sailed	One

This photograph of the back of the bridge of the *Musashi* is of particular value to modelmakers. Note the bracing on the back of the main director rangefinder, which was fitted to *Musashi* before *Yamato*. The top of the director is painted white as an aid to aircraft recognition, marking it out as a vessel of the IJN.

■ GUN CHARACTERISTICS

	46cm (18.1in)	15.5cm (6.1in)	12.7cm (5in)	25mm	13.2mm
GUN					
Bore (inches)	18.1in	6.1in	5in	0.984in	0.52in
Designation	Type 94	3rd Year Type	Type 89 Model A-1-3	Type 96	Type 93
Length in cals	45	60	40	60	76
Weight incl breech	162.4 tons	12.5 tons	3.05 tons	94.8lb	43.7lb
Length oa	831.9in	378.5in	208.03in	90.39in	55.5in
Shell weight	3219lb (Type 91 AP)	123lb	50.7lb	8.82oz	1.57–1.83oz
Charge weight	794lb	43lb	8.77lb	3.6–3.88oz	0.53oz
Muzzle velocity	2559–2575fs	3018–3035fs	2362–2379fs	2953fs	2641fs
Approximate life	200–250 EFC	250–300 EFC	800–1500 EFC	12,000 EFC	?
Maximum range	45,960yds	29,960yds	16,075yds	8200yds	6560yds
@ °elevation	45°	45°			
Ceiling			30,970ft @ 90°	18,040ft @ 85°	13,065ft @ 85°
Max Rate of fire	2rpm	5rpm	14rpm; 8 sustained	200–260rpm	425–475rpm
MOUNTING					
Type	Triple	Triple	Twin	Triple	Twin
Weight	2470 tons	177 tons	28.5 tons	3970lb	692lb
Diam of roller path	42.81ft	18ft 9in	7.48ft	–	–
Between gun axes	137.8in	61in	26.77in	–	–
Max elevating speed	8°/second	10°/second	12°/second; later 16°	18°/second	
Max training speed	2°/second	6°/second	6°/second; later 16°	12°/second	
Max/Min Elevation	+45° to -5°	+55° to -10°	+90° to -8°	+90° to -10°	
AMMUNITION					
Normal allocation	100rpg	150rpg	300rpg	2000rpg	2500rpg

AP = armour piercing; fs = feet per second; EFC = Equivalent full charge; rpm = rounds per minute; rpg = rounds per gun (barrel)

The bridge tower of the *Yamato* class was quite unlike that on any other class of battleship – a massive structure that resembled a medieval Japanese castle interpreted in steel. This image of *Musashi* was taken in June or July of 1943.

Career History

The surprise attack on the US Navy at Pearl Harbor by the Imperial Japanese Navy on 7 December 1941 not only caught the Americans off-guard but also the citizens of Japan and the yard workers constructing the *Yamato* class battleships. *Yamato* herself was commissioned on 16 December 1941 and became part of the First Battleship Division as third ship, with *Nagato* (flagship) and *Mutsu*. They would train together during the remainder of December and on into February 1942. On 12 February *Yamato* became the Flagship of the Combined Fleet, under the command of Admiral Yamamoto.

During this time work on the *Musashi* was pushed forward as quickly as possible, and the Mitsubishi Dock Yard assigned more workers to accelerate her construction. In the meantime the IJN was seriously reconsidering the construction of any more battleships. The successful attack upon the US Navy at Pearl Harbor and the sinking of the Royal Navy capital ships HMS *Prince of Wales* and *Repulse* dramatically emphasised the increasing potency of air power, and suggested a need for more aircraft carriers. In January 1942, work was ordered to be stopped on Warships No 110 and No 111, the modified *Yamato* class

This view from the rear of the bridge tower of the *Musashi* looks down through the mainmast rigging to the aircraft handling deck. This deck had a concrete surface layer. The photo was taken in June or July of 1942.

battleships, until the strategic direction of the IJN could be determined. By February, work resumed, but at a much reduced pace in an effort to finish the hull for No 110 in one year.

The *Yamato* remained in Japanese waters for the next few months, training her gun crews with particularly thorough drills, made necessary by the characteristics of the new monster 18.1in main armament. These weapons required a new approach to firing because their muzzle blast was so powerful it would shatter anything in its path. Crew members had to take complete cover, anti-aircraft gun mounts had to be covered with blast-proof shields, vents had to be faced away from the direction of discharge, and any optical devices had to be protected. Members of the future crew of

her sister-ship *Musashi* were also aboard for this training.

On its first operational sortie *Yamato*, as the Imperial Japanese Navy Fleet Flagship, departed Japanese waters with a massive task force bound for Midway Island. The planned assault on that US Navy base was to be the next step in the Japanese advance across the Pacific Ocean, but in the ensuing Battle of Midway the US Navy won a decisive victory over the IJN in what turned out to be a massive duel between aircraft carriers alone. All four of the aircraft carriers in the IJN's primary strike force were sunk, but the greater loss was that of the air crews from those carriers – a loss that the IJN was never to recover from. The *Yamato* was with the main invasion force, which turned back after the loss of the

A front view of the massive bridge tower of the *Musashi*, taken at the same time as the previous photo. Note the tripod aerial support on the forward 6.1in gun, which was rigged with a swivel atop the tripod, so the yardarm remained athwartships when the turret trained.

This view of the back of the bridge tower on *Yamato* was taken while the ship was under construction (it is dated 20 September 1941). This image makes an interesting comparison with the similar view of *Musashi* reproduced earlier, pointing up the slight differences between the sisters.

A close-up view of the Type 7 'Gata' antenna for the Type 21 radar system. This system could range on a group of aircraft or a large warship, at a distance of 75 miles, a single aircraft or destroyer at 43 miles. This radar system was developed in Japan independently of foreign technology.

Another view of the back of the main battery rangefinder and the upper bridge tower of *Musashi*. She was either built with the rangefinder bracing or had it added just after completion. *Musashi* was also commissioned with the Type 7 radar antenna atop the rangefinder for the Type 21 air and surface search radar system.

Opposite: This close-up of the *Yamato* is a cropped enlargement from the well-known view of the ship under construction during her fitting-out period (a colourised version of the whole image is on page 47). Even though the warship is not completed, there is a wealth of detail that model-builders will find most useful.

aircraft carrier force, and the entire operation was cancelled, with the fleet returning to Japan.

This battle changed the direction of planning within the Imperial Japanese Navy. There was a drastic and immediate need for more aircraft carriers after the traumatic losses at Midway, and it was at this time that the IJN made the decision to convert Warship No 110 to an aircraft carrier. The hull was about 50 per cent complete, with the propulsion machinery installed, which enabled the Yokosuka Navy Yard to make the conversion with less effort. The vessel was then given the name *Shinano*, but her completion as a carrier was never to be realized, as she was torpedoed by the USN submarine *Archerfish* on 29 November 1944 while being relocated to avoid destruction from American bombing of the Japanese home islands. At the time the ship's fitting-out was far from complete, but she remained afloat for seven hours after four torpedo hits, barely assisted by the poorly organised efforts of an inexperienced crew, which must have been attributable to the basically sound underwater protection system. Also during the summer of 1942 the construction of Warship No 111 was halted and the 30 per cent complete hull was scrapped. Another battleship of a modified *Yamato* design (actually a modified No 110 design), known as Warship No 797, scheduled to start construction in the summer of 1942, was cancelled and was never laid down.

At this time the construction of the *Musashi* was delayed by at least three months due to the decision to fit her with flagship accommodation. In order to finish fitting her out and to run trials, she had been moved from Nagasaki to Kure. *Musashi* was commissioned into the IJN on 5 August 1942 and was assigned to Battleship Division One with *Yamato*, *Nagato* and *Mutsu*. However, *Musashi* remained at Kure for the next five months for additional fitting out and extensive trials

and training of her crew in the Inland Sea. In September 1942 *Musashi* received the IJN Type 21 radar, with its massive antenna atop the main gun director arms. She also received four additional 25mm mounts on her main deck fore and aft of the wing triple 6in secondary turrets, both port and starboard. During this time, in August 1942, the *Yamato* sailed for the IJN forward base of Truk, in the Caroline Islands, about 1000 miles north of the Solomon Island chain. The *Yamato* was stationed at Truk with other IJN battleships of the *Kongo* class, who were very active during this time with the Guadalcanal campaign, but *Yamato* would remain idle for the next few months.

During the month of December 1942 *Musashi* exercised in the Inland Sea with the battleships *Nagato*, *Yamashiro* and *Fuso*. When she was finished with her training and post-trial refits, she was transferred to Truk, on 22 January 1943. Admiral Yamamoto then transferred his flag from the *Yamato* to the *Musashi* on 11 February 1943, but both battleships remained idle through April and into May 1943, even though the battleships *Kongo* and *Haruna*, also based at Truk, were still very active with the Guadalcanal campaign. On 18 April USAAF P-38 fighter aircraft, acting upon code breaking information, intercepted Admiral Yamamoto's 'Betty' bomber transport aircraft and shot it and another down, killing the IJN fleet commander and most of his staff. By early May Admiral Koga had replaced Yamamoto as Fleet Commander of the Imperial Japanese Navy Combined Fleet. *Musashi* departed Truk bound for Yokosuka on 17 May 1943, eventually making a call at Tokyo, carrying the ashes of Admiral Yamamoto for his state funeral. *Yamato* had departed Truk one week prior to *Musashi*, bound for Kure Navy Yard.

In June of 1943, *Musashi* was cleaned up and prepared for an inspection tour by Navy Yard officials. The Japanese Emperor Hirohito visited the *Musashi* for a festive dinner and a tour of the entire battleship, including the crew's quarters and the anti-aircraft defence position on the upper bridge. This was the one and only time the Japanese Emperor visited either one of his two super battleships.

During the month of July 1943 both *Yamato* and *Musashi* underwent a refit and upgrade at the Kure Navy Yard. Both battleships were dry-docked for hull cleaning and repainting, and the new paint job was extended to the entire superstructure and armament. *Yamato* received her first radar system, IJN Type 21, with its massive antenna atop the main director arms. *Musashi* was fitted with her second radar, the IJN Type 22, on both the port and starboard bridge top. *Yamato* received four additional 25mm AA mounts on her main deck fore and aft of the wing triple 6in turrets, both port and starboard. By the end of July 1943, with their refits and modifications complete, *Musashi* departed for Truk, followed by *Yamato* in mid-August.

On 18 September 1943 American forces attacked the Japanese-held island fortress of Tarawa with carrier-borne aircraft, in what was a prelude to the invasion of that island. In response to this the IJN Combined Fleet sortied from Truk for the Eniwetok atoll. This force included the battleships *Yamato* and *Nagato*, two fleet carriers, a light carrier, heavy and light cruisers and destroyers. *Musashi*, *Fuso*, *Kongo* and *Haruna* remained at Truk in reserve. The operation ended in anti-climax: after not making contact with the US fleet, *Yamato* and the IJN Fleet returned to Truk by the end of September.

In October the IJN was convinced that an attack by US forces upon Wake Island was imminent. Admiral Koga sortied with *Yamato*, *Musashi*, *Nagato*, *Fuso*, *Kongo*, *Haruna*, two fleet carriers, one light carrier, a large force of heavy and light cruisers and numerous destroyers in an effort to intercept the US fleet. Admiral Koga stationed the Task Force 250nm miles south of Wake Island, but was unable to make contact with the US Navy, and the IJN fleet returned to Truk at the end of October after another unsuccessful attempt to engage the enemy. As it turned out, the American Navy then raided Wake and the Marshall Islands in early November after waiting for the Japanese Navy to retire from the area. Unsuspected by the Japanese, the Americans were intercepting and reading IJN coded transmissions, which made them better able to anticipate most of the moves made by the Japanese Navy.

Yamato departed Truk on 12 December 1943, as the main escort for a force of two fleet carriers, troop transports and destroyers, bound for Yokosuka, Japan. After reaching Japan, *Yamato* would turn around, and with destroyers, sail back to Truk, herself loaded with troops and supplies. As she was approaching Truk on the return voyage, on 25 December, she

was hit by one torpedo from a spread of four from the USN submarine USS *Skate*. The detonation of this torpedo on *Yamato*'s starboard side, abreast the No 3 turret, crushed some 30m of her anti-torpedo blister, causing 3000 tons of water to flood into the No 3 turret magazine and into one of the adjacent engine rooms. More importantly, *Yamato*'s side armour failed due to a flawed joint between the upper and lower belts. Counter-flooding added 2000 tons of water to reduce the list and enable her to continue on to Truk, where she arrived the next day. *Yamato* underwent emergency repairs at Truk for twelve days in preparation to departing for Kure for more extensive repairs on 10 January 1944. *En route, Yamato* was spotted by two US Navy submarines, but they were too far away to make a successful attack, and she arrived safely at Kure on 16 January 1944.

Yamato was immediately dry-docked at Kure to repair her failed side belt armour

and the torpedo damage, which took until 3 February 1944. *Yamato* then went to the fitting-out pier for a major refit and modifications. She had both the port and starboard triple 6in secondary gun mounts removed and the superstructure extended outward to accommodate additional AA weapons: six twin 5in DP gun mounts were installed, three port and three starboard, on the new superstructure. Twelve triple 25mm AA mounts were also added, six port and six starboard, as well as two additional 25mm directors, IJN Type 13 radar on the mainmast and Type 22 radar on the port and starboard bridge top. *Yamato* completed these major alterations in early April 1944, at which time she ran trials in the Inland Sea until late in the month.

During this time *Musashi* remained at Truk, with other units of the Combined Fleet, until on 4 February 1944 an overflight by American PB4Y patrol bombers, alerted the IJN that an air raid by US carrier-based planes was imminent. *Musashi*, along with other warships, departed for Yokosuka, Japan, on 10 February. Truk was then attacked by US carrier aircraft for two days, 17–18 February, in what was one of the most successful carrier operations of the Second World War. The Japanese lost two light cruisers, three destroyers and thirty-five other naval and merchant supply vessels, as well as over 250 aircraft destroyed on the ground. *Musashi* arrived at Yokosuka on 15 February 1944, loaded troops and supplies and departed for Palau on 24 February, with Admiral Koga aboard.

En route to Palau *Musashi* and her escorting three destroyers encountered a massive typhoon. Army munitions, fuel and vehicles stowed on the deck of *Musashi* were washed overboard or jettisoned during this storm. The Japanese Army troops aboard *Musashi* were crowded below with her crew, which made living conditions extremely difficult. The battleship was forced to slow to 6 knots to allow the three destroyers to keep station with her. After arriving at Palau, 29 February 1944, *Musashi* remained there until 29 March, when due to the impending American air raids, she departed for the Philippines. Just before, on 28 March, Admiral Koga decided not to travel aboard *Musashi*, but rather to travel by aircraft to the Philippines.

At almost 6pm on the day *Musashi* departed Palau, she was hit by a single torpedo, just as she cleared the channel to the open sea. Luckily for her, only this one found its target out of a spread of six fired by the American submarine USS *Tunny*. The hit, in the port bow, caused 3000 tons of water to flood many forward compartments. She was forced to stop to make emergency repairs, which lasted well into the night, but once the patching-up was deemed adequate, she headed for a new destination, Kure.

An example of the IJN twin 5in open mount that was the standard heavy AA weapon installed on battleships, carriers and cruisers.

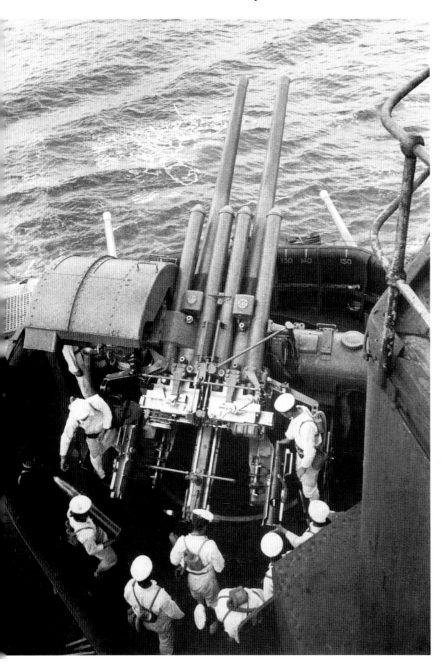

The standard triple 25mm open AA mount with a crew of nine men.

Admiral Koga and his staff may have felt lucky to avoid the set-back, and on the night of 31 March 1944 they took off from Palau in a pair of four-engined Kawanishi 'Emily' flying boats, bound for the Philippines. However, they ran into a fierce typhoon, both planes going down: only Admiral Koga's Chief of Staff, Vice Admiral Fukudome survived, found at sea days later by the Japanese Army.

When *Musashi* arrived at Kure on 3 April 1944 she was dry-docked right away to repair the torpedo damage to her hull. It was planned that *Musashi* was to receive the same major modifications applied to her sister-ship *Yamato*, but there was a shortage of material and time. Her super-structure was modified in similar fashion to that of *Yamato*, but she was only to receive temporary 25mm triple AA gun mounts in place of the proposed 5in twin mounts. Additional 25mm gun directors were installed, as well as the IJN Type 13 radar antenna on the mainmast. *Musashi* ran her post-refit trials from the end of April to early May, and then sailed with six light carriers and destroyers for Okinawa on 10 May 1944.

Yamato had left Kure on 21 April 1944 for Manila in the Philippines with a load of troops and supplies. She would stop there just long enough to disembark the troops and supplies for that base and then departed for Singapore on the 28th. Upon her arrival at Singapore (1 May 1944), *Yamato* was designated as Flagship of Battleship Division One, Admiral Ugaki transferring from *Nagato*, which had been temporary flagship while *Yamato* and

Musashi were in Japanese waters. On 11 May *Yamato* steamed for the IJN anchorage at Tawi Tawi, off the northern coast of Borneo, dividing the Sulu and Celebes Seas, with BatDiv 2 and 3, arriving on 14 May 1944. Meanwhile, *Musashi* arrived from Okinawa on 16 May, joining BatDiv 1 and Admiral Ozawa's Mobile Fleet, consisting of BatDiv 1's *Yamato*, *Musashi* and *Nagato*, BatDiv 2's *Fuso*, and BatDiv 3's *Kongo* and *Haruna*. All six of these Japanese battleships participated, with cruisers and destroyers of the Mobile Fleet, in battle exercises and joint gunnery drills in the Sulu Sea during the period of late May and into early June 1944. During one of these gunnery drills *Yamato* and *Musashi* shot to a range of 22 miles.

While this was happening the American Navy staged an invasion of the island of Biak, on the north-western coast of New Guinea on 27 May 1944. In response the IJN Mobile Fleet at Tawi Tawi sailed in three groups between 30 May and 11 June. *Yamato* and *Musashi*, with cruisers and destroyers, sortied on 10 June, but soon sighted a submarine periscope and in the confusion of wild manoeuvring the two super-battleships almost ran into each other, *Musashi* coming to a complete stop to avoid colliding with *Yamato*. This operation was cancelled, and by 17 June *Yamato* and *Musashi* had joined with other units of the Mobile Fleet to counter the US Navy's latest offensive, the invasions of Guam and Saipan in the Mariana Islands. In the opening phase of the resulting Battle of the Philippine Sea the Japanese Navy launched hundreds of carrier-borne

■ ANTI-AIRCRAFT ALTERATIONS TO THE *YAMATO* CLASS

Yamato July 1943 (total: 12 x 5in + 36 x 25mm)

Four 25mm triple open mounts added on weather deck abreast superstructure

Yamato April 1944 (total: 24 x 5in + 98 x 25mm)

Six 5in twin open mounts added on superstructure

Twelve 25mm triple enclosed mounts added on superstructure and weather deck

Twenty-six 25mm single open mounts added on weather deck

Musashi April 1944 (total: 12 x 5in + 115 x 25mm)

Eighteen 25mm triple open mounts added on superstructure and weather deck

Twenty-five 25mm single open mounts added on weather deck

Yamato July 1944 (total: 24 x 5in + 113 x 25mm)

Five 25mm triple open mounts added

Musashi July 1944 (total: 12 x 5in + 130 x 25mm)

Five 25mm triple open mounts on weather deck

Yamato March 1945 (total: 24 x 5in + 152 x 25mm)

Six 25mm triple enclosed mounts added on weather deck

Fifteen 25mm triple open mounts added on superstructure

Twenty-four 25mm single open mounts removed from weather deck

aircraft to attack the US Navy invasion fleet, but were utterly destroyed in a one-sided engagement that became known as the 'Great Marianas Turkey Shoot'. The defeated IJN Mobile Fleet then retired north, first to Okinawa to refuel, then back to various naval bases in Japan, *Yamato* and *Musashi* to Kure Navy Yard, arriving on 29 June 1944.

Both super-battleships received a refit while at Kure during this time. They were fitted with five triple and five single 25mm AA open mounts on the main deck at the fore and aft ends of the superstructure. It was known that *Yamato* had some of, or possibly the entire main deck planking replaced at that time. Both warships would complete this refit about 7 July 1944.

The Mobile Fleet departed Kure for Okinawa on 9 July, *Yamato* and *Musashi* steaming in company with *Nagato*, *Kongo*, cruisers and destroyers. After refuelling at Okinawa, they split into two groups, with Group A (*Yamato*, *Musashi*, cruisers and destroyers) departing Okinawa, 10 July, for the Lingga Roads anchorage, just south of Singapore. *En route*, Group A then split into two parts with the super-battleships dropping anchor at Lingga and the cruisers and destroyers at Singapore, both arriving on 17 July 1944.

The majority of the Imperial Japanese Navy was concentrated at the Singapore anchorages in an effort to counter the American forces in what the Japanese suspected to be their next assault, the Philippine Islands. *Yamato*, and *Musashi*, with *Nagato*, *Kongo* and *Haruna*, all battleships, participated in gunnery drills both day and night, with the addition of radar guided fire-control systems. These battleships and other units of the Imperial Japanese Navy would train, practice and undergo maintenance while based at both the Lingga Roads and Singapore anchorages and naval yard, July through mid-October 1944. Also during this time, both *Yamato* and *Musashi* had their main decks painted a very dark grey; the tinting for this paint was the soot from their funnels. During September 1944 *Musashi* had her vertical surfaces painted a very dark grey from former Royal Navy paint stocks found at Singapore after the British surrender.

On 18 October 1944 *Yamato* and *Musashi*, with *Nagato*, *Fuso*, *Yamashiro*, *Kongo* and *Haruna*, sailed from the Lingga Roads anchorage for Brunei Bay, on the north-western coast of the island of Borneo, arriving there on 20 October. At Brunei Bay the IJN Fleet refuelled and resupplied for one day and prepared for an operation dubbed 'Sho-I-Go' (Victory). They would sortie from Brunei Bay on 22 October in two large task forces, heading for what was to become the largest naval battle of all time – Leyte Gulf.

Continued on page 51

A close-up of a triple 25mm enclosed AA mount on the *Musashi*. These mounts were enclosed to protect the gun crews from the blast of the 18.1in main guns.

Reference Material

Both of the books pictured to the right are perfect for model builders looking for background information before building models of the *Yamato* class battleships. The book to the near right is one from the Gakken series, of which there are several on the *Yamato* class. They are a mixture of both history and models. The book to the far right is a modeller's guide to the *Yamato* class from Model Art. It covers all aspects of modelling the *Yamato* class at all time frames and all model scales. Both can be highly recommended.

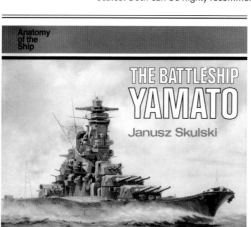

This is the best book on the structure and details of the *Yamato*. Although it could be used to build a model of her sister-ship, the *Musashi*, you would need to consult other references to find out about the differences between the two warships. The drawings in this book on the *Yamato* are, simply put, the best available, anywhere. They are extensive enough that one could build the most detailed model in almost any scale, even up to 1/48! Also included is a good history on the vessel, but the few photos included are not reproduced to the highest quality. However, if you are interested in any aspect of *Yamato* class battleships, this book is a must-have.

Another fantastic book by Model Art Publications, this one is from their series of 'Super Illustration' books, offering a wealth of detail drawings of all of the hull, superstructure, weapons, fittings, etc – all in isometric views. The value of an isometric view compared to a conventional two-dimensional plan or elevation is that it represents its subject as a three-dimensional object, allowing the model builder to visualise in the round what is drawn in a flat illustration. There are over 100 illustrations in this book in the isometric format, making it a superb supplement to the Anatomy book on the *Yamato*. As with that book, if you are interested in the *Yamato*, this book is another essential addition to your library.

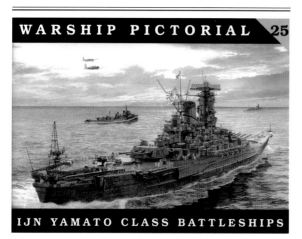

One of the few English-language books on the *Yamato* class containing a large number of photographs, this book also features a few drawings of these warships, as well as drawings of interior cross-sections, aircraft and a colour illustration of *Yamato* upon commissioning. A tabular record of movements is provided for the history of the two largest battleships in the world, as well as the same for their sister-ship, *Shinano*, that was converted to an aircraft carrier. For photographic reference, with 90 per cent of all known and existing *Yamato* class photographs, this is certainly the best value for money.

For the *Yamato* class battleship enthusiast looking for the highest quality photographic reproduction in a nice coffee-table size book, this is definitely the book. From Diamond Publishing in Japan, it is easy to obtain through Hobby Link Japan on the Internet. The photos are presented in a large format with the best print quality that has ever been published to date. Not every known photograph of the *Yamato* class is in this book, but the images presented are inspiring. This is a book for the serious Imperial Japanese Navy and *Yamato* class enthusiast.

Model Kits

There have probably been more model kits of the *Yamato* class battleships produced than any other warship – more than USS *Missouri*, or a *Fletcher* class destroyer, or even the hugely popular *Bismarck*. It is possible to find a kit of this type of warship in almost any scale imaginable, so this volume will only cover those that this author deems to be of better value to the model builder. The criteria here are quality, accuracy and cost of the model kits available on the market.

GHQ *YAMATO* AND *MUSASHI*   1/2400 scale

This model is offered by GHQ in the naval wargaming scale of 1/2400. These models come unpainted and will require minor assembly. A *Yamato* class battleship measures out to 4.3125 inches in overall length in this scale, making it a good size for table-top naval wargaming.

NEPTUN *YAMATO* AND *MUSASHI*   1/1250 scale

Pictured here are two examples of the fine metal models offered by Navis Neptun Models of Germany. Although models of this scale can be used for wargaming, these models are detailed enough for display and as such have become very collectable. The image below is Neptun's standard issue, this one of *Musashi*, while the image above of their *Yamato* offering is from their upgrade line of models. These models come correctly painted and also, in the case of the latter series, fully rigged. The quality of the workmanship in this upgrade series is absolutely amazing in an off-the-shelf model and really has to be seen to be believed. For the money, the upgrade models from Neptun are the best that this author has ever seen in any commercially available offering in 1/1250 scale.

TAKARA G-MIX *YAMATO*

1/700 scale

■ Due for release in September 2009 in the Takara G-Mix Ground Sailing Model Series is this 1/700 *Yamato*. Advance information describes it as an infrared control waterline model that 'sails on the ground', with three forward speeds, and one astern, with the top speed equivalent to 28 knots. It can be steered to port and starboard, the turrets turn, gun barrels elevate, and the rangefinder on the bridge turns with the gun turrets. It has a sound control system, steaming, gun fire, and whistle, and it also has running lights.

■ Report and photos by courtesy of the **J-Modelworks** website.

FUJIMI *YAMATO* AND *MUSASHI*

1/700 scale

■ The Fujimi Model Co of Japan is one of the oldest in the plastic model industry and was one of the original members of the 'Water Line Series' consortium. It has recently issued two new kits of the *Yamato* class in 1/700 scale. The kit pictured is of the *Musashi* in her appearance as commissioned, August 1942. This kit is a vast improvement over the castings of old from this company, which was often regarded as the poor relation of the consortium. The finesse of the detail on the kit parts is quite good and the accuracy of the model overall is also excellent. An as-built *Yamato* can also be constructed from this kit, and as it is rare to see either of these vessels in this configuration, this is a welcome addition to the line. Highly recommended.

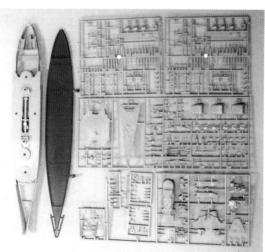

TAMIYA *YAMATO* AND *MUSASHI*

The Tamiya Model Co of Japan was possibly the founder of the 'Water Line Series' consortium and is one of the oldest plastic model manufacturers in Japan. It released both *Yamato* and *Musashi* kits in this scale back in 1998 with new-mould tooling. The quality of these new castings is superb, possibly the best in 1/700 scale, with a level of detail in this small scale that is second to none. Accuracy is quite good and the instructions are in an exploded isometric view that makes assembly very easy to perform. The painting instructions, pictured here, are the best from any manufacturer. The *Yamato* kit, illustrated here, is of her April 1945 configuration, while the *Musashi* kit depicts her in August 1942. With this model kit it would also be possible to back-date the *Yamato* to her October 1944 configuration if one desires. Both kits are fantastic and highly recommended.

FUJIMI *YAMATO*   1/500 scale

The Fujimi Model Co made a surprise announcement at the 48th Shizuoka Hobby Show in 2009, revealing a new 1/500 kit of *Yamato* (1945), the development of which they had conducted in strict secrecy. The older Nichimo *Yamato* and *Musashi* in 1/500 were quite simplistic and not very good quality model kits, so this new offering from Fujimi will make 1/500 scale builders very happy – in Japan the serious builders of 1/500 scale have a very exclusive club in which they promote their scale. Earlier kits of other battleships were mainly resin productions, so this new plastic kit may help to rejuvenate the 1/500 scale section of the hobby. These exhibits were the rapid prototyping and the actual styrene test shot parts of the hull. Release date is to be the autumn of 2009.

■ Report and photos by courtesy of the **J-Modelworks** website.

TAMIYA *YAMATO* AND *MUSASHI* 1/350 scale

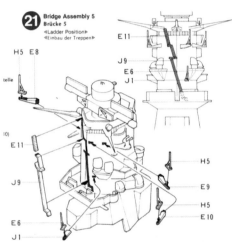

The Tamiya Model Co of Japan has produced one of, if not the, best models of the *Yamato* class that has ever been manufactured by any one company. So much so that these kits, first released back in the early 1980s, have stood the test for all these years – and not another *Yamato* kit has been produced in this scale by another manufacturer since. They are very nice model kits indeed, but they are not quite perfect. With the discovery of new information about these two mysterious giants, there are a few modifications needed, but this can be done with the addition of detail parts from aftermarket companies like Lion

Pictured above are all of the plastic parts for the Tamiya 1/350 *Musashi* model kit.

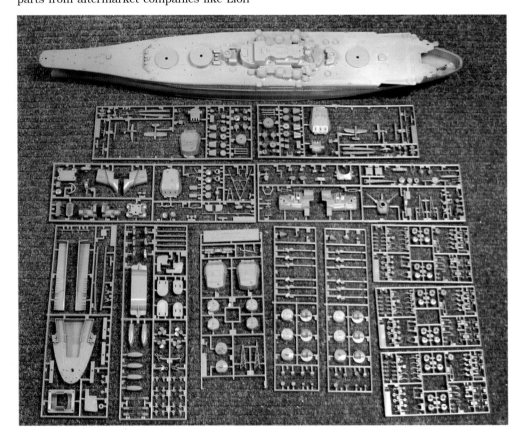

Roar and others. I personally wish that Tamiya would make an early version of either of these two, as well as a *Shinano*, as both a carrier and a battleship, but in 1/350

these kits will build into a very impressive model. The detail is fantastic, instructions superb, fitment top-notch, accuracy good, and both can be highly recommended.

ARII/OTAKI *YAMATO* AND *MUSASHI*   1/250 scale

This kit, originally put out by Otaki of Japan, is now available under the Arii name, also of Japan. *Yamato* in this scale measures out to 41 inches in length, making for a good-sized model. The quality of the kit is good, but it was released back in the late 1970s, and with more up to date

information available on the *Yamato*s, the kit is now a little dated. With the set of Gold Medal Models photo-etch brass details, however, it still can be made into a stunning replica of either *Yamato* or *Musashi*. The kit is a little hard to find, but well worth the trouble.

NICHIMO *YAMATO* AND *MUSASHI* — 1/200 scale

■ Nichimo Models of Japan first introduced this kit of the *Yamato* in 1/200 some time back in the late 1970s. Along with it, they produced two *Akizuki* and two *Kagero* class destroyers from the Second World War period in the same scale. This model is massive, but still affordable on the average budget. The detail is good to average, and because of the date of manufacture, there are a few inaccuracies, but these are all correctable with a little scratch-building. This model comes with the hardware to motorise the model, or if one chooses, to be built as a full-hull display model. The gearbox for motorisation even provides for the proper counter-rotation of the propeller shafts. With the addition of the Gold Medal Models photo-etch detail parts, some corrections, and the Shinsengumi replacement wood decking, this will build into a very impressive model. As of the date of this publication additional detail parts are under development.

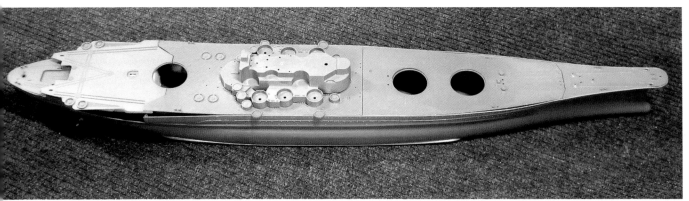

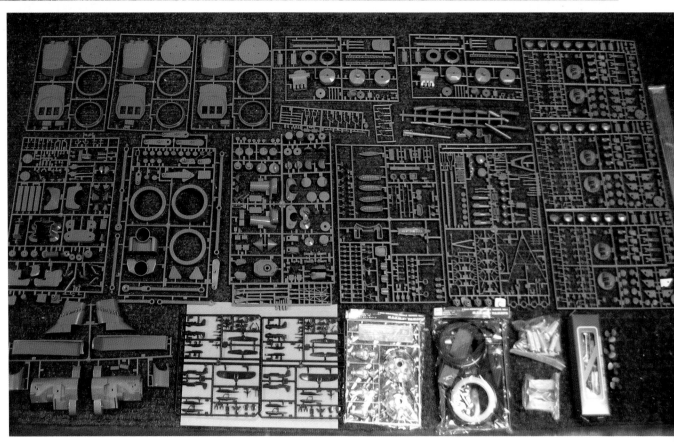

SOAR ART *YAMATO* 1/144 scale

Soar Art Workshop of Hong Kong produces this massive model of the *Yamato* in her April 1945, final voyage, configuration. In this scale *Yamato* measures out to an impressive 72 inches overall length. One can see from both of the images presented here that this is a very detailed model. This model is available for display purposes only, but I am sure that Soar Art must be contemplating the release of a radio control version in the future. If you have the financial independence and the space required to display this beast, then this is the *Yamato* model for you.

SCALE SHIPYARD AND FLEETSCALE *YAMATO* 1/96 scale

Both of these companies manufacture a fibreglass hull for the *Yamato* in 1/96 scale that measures an astounding 108 inches in length and 16 inches in beam. Scale Shipyard of the USA only makes a hull, but Fleetscale of the UK produces a slightly better detailed hull and also makes a wide variety of fittings and weapons, as well as the basic superstructure and funnel. I believe that these are currently the largest kits manufactured of the *Yamato* class battleships, although at one time there was a hull offered in 1/72 scale. This is a very popular scale for radio-controlled warships, as the image to the left illustrates. Short of scratch-building a *Yamato* class battleship in a larger scale, these hulls and parts are the best way to go, if one desires a very large model of these warships. Of course these can also be constructed for display purposes only.

Model Detail Accessories

There are vast numbers of detail accessories available to up-grade or even convert kits to another version of the same vessel or a sister-ship. In fact, this area of the market is expanding at a dramatic rate, with many new detail sets being released on a regular basis. Furthermore, the quality of the products coming out is outstanding and every new release seems to push the standard even higher. The listing that follows gives a brief summary of the most significant offerings, but for further details, including contact information, on any of these companies, see the website list on page 64 at the end of this book.

GOLD MEDAL MODELS
1/700, 1/350, 1/250 & 1/200 scales

Gold Medal Models has been in the ship model accessory business longer than any other company. As their name suggests, their award-winning photo-etch product sets a benchmark against which all

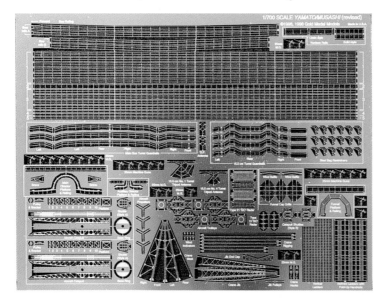

other etch products will be judged. Their sets for the *Yamato* class battleships are displayed here. These sets are available in 1/700, 1/350, 1/250 and 1/200 scales. The set to the left is for 1/350, while the set below is for 1/200 scale. Some of the multitude of items provided are as follows: railing in several styles, including chain with a realistic 'droop', and solid types with pre-shaped sections for upswept bow and special sections for gun turrets; vertical and inclined ladders; aircraft catapults, aircraft handling trolleys, crane, and propellers; Type 13 and Type 21 radar, gun director details, RDF antennas, funnel cap grills, 15.5cm (6.1in) turret blast bag restrainers, watertight doors, and wind direction indicators. There are many other details included, too many to list. Again, any products from this company are top quality and highly recommended.

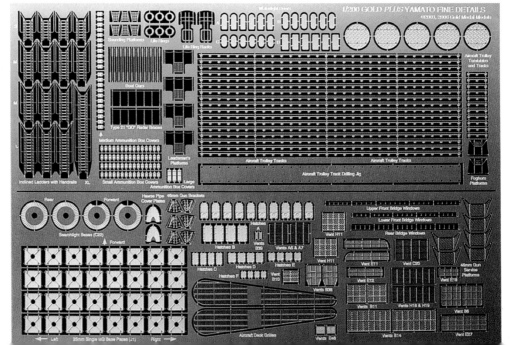

TOMS MODELWORKS
1/700, 1/500, 1/350, & 1/200 scales

Tom's Modelworks from the USA has an extensive line of photo-etch detail items for the IJN in 1/700, 1/500, 1/350 and 1/200 scales. Items range from the ship's doors, pictured here, to anchors, cable reels, a *Yamato* class set in 1/700, life lines, portholes in 1/350 and others. Another product that can be highly recommended.

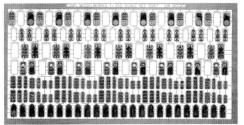

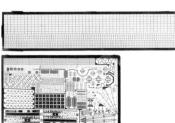

EDUARD
1/700 & 1/350 scales

Eduard Model Accessories from the Czech Republic is another world leader in photo-etch model accessories. Pictured here are images of their set for the Tamiya 1/350 *Musashi* kit in her October 1944 configuration. Eduard offers sets for the *Yamato* class battleships in 1/700 and 1/350 scales. They also offer sets of pre-painted photo-etch figures in both of the above-mentioned scales and a multitude of other products that are all very good.

LION ROAR

1/700 & 1/350 scales

Lion Roar is a relative newcomer to the model accessory business, but they have made a big splash with their fantastic product line. Pictured here is their set for the *Yamato* in 1/350. This set contains thirteen sheets of photo-etch, four brass propellers, 5in, 6in, and 18in brass gun barrels, and even anchor chain. The quality of the product is as good as the very best on the market. If one is constructing the ultimate *Yamato*, then is a set to seriously consider.

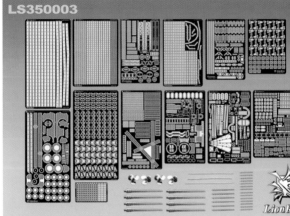

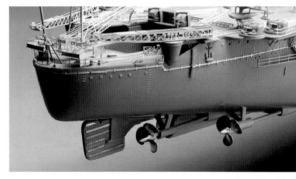

VETERAN MODELS

1/350 scale

Veteran Models of Hong Kong is without doubt the most amazing 1/350 model accessory company that this author has ever discovered. Their use of computer aided mould design has paid huge dividends in terms of some of the best detail items on the market today, as can be seen by the sample images of their offering illustrated on this page. All of the items pictured here are applicable to both the *Yamato* and the *Musashi*, and would be an enormous complement to any of the photo-etch detail sets displayed in this book. When looking at the product in these images, one would think that they are looking at detail accessories in 1/100 scale, but no, these really are available in 1/350 scale in this level of finesse. They are made through computer aided design, from a catalyzing liquid polymer, in a process known as stereo lithography. As the success of their sales increases, we will, no doubt see a lot more of this amazing product from this company

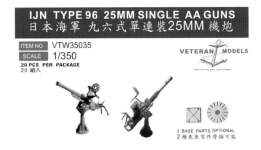

IJN TYPE 96 25MM SINGLE AA GUNS
日本海軍 九六式單連裝25MM 機炮

ITEM NO VTW35035
SCALE 1/350
20 PCS PER PACKAGE
20 組入

VETERAN MODELS

2 BASE PARTS OPTIONAL
2 種底座零件替換可能

VETERAN MODELS WE BRING YOU REAL SHIPS

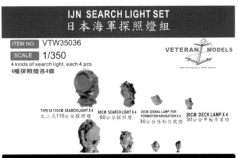

IJN SEARCH LIGHT SET
日本海軍探照燈組

ITEM NO VTW35036
SCALE 1/350
4 kinds of search light, each 4 pcs
4種探照燈各4個

VETERAN MODELS

TYPE 92 110CM SEARCH LIGHT X 4
九二式110公分探照燈

60CM SEARCH LIGHT X 4
60公分探照燈

30CM SIGNAL LAMP FOR FORMATION NAVIGATION X 4
30公分隊形紅號燈

30CM DECK LAMP X 4
30公分甲板作業燈

VETERAN MODELS WE BRING YOU REAL SHIPS

in the future. All of these products will also work to detail any other Imperial Japanese Navy warship that was outfitted with the same weaponry. Most highly recommended!

IJN TYPE 96 25MM TWIN AA GUNS
日本海軍 九六式雙連裝25MM 機炮

ITEM NO VTW35034
SCALE 1/350
10 PCS PER PACKAGE
10 組入

VETERAN MODELS

VETERAN MODELS WE BRING YOU REAL SHIPS

IJN 6CM, 8CM, 12CM BINOCULAR SETS (WITH VOICE PIPES)
日本海軍6公分、8公分、12公分望遠鏡組（包含通話筒）

ITEM NO VTW35032
SCALE 1/350

6cm Binocular x 10   12cm Binocular x20
Voice Pipe x 40   8cm Binocular x20
Binocular with Signal Lamp x 4
110cm Serach Light Controller x4
Binocular with Infra-Red Message Transmitter x4

VETERAN MODELS WE BRIING YOU REAL SHIPS

TYPE 89 12.7CM 40CAL AA GUNS
日本海軍 八九式12.7公分高角砲
（含金屬砲管&信管秒時調整器）

ITEM NO VTW35031
SCALE 1/350
4PCS PER PACKAGE

(Fuse Second Controller & Brass Barrels included)

VETERAN MODELS WE BRIING YOU REAL SHIPS

IJN TYPE 96 25MM TRIPLE AA GUNS
日本海軍 九六式三連裝25MM 機炮

ITEM NO VTW35033
SCALE 1/350
10 PCS PER PACKAGE
10 組入

VETERAN MODELS

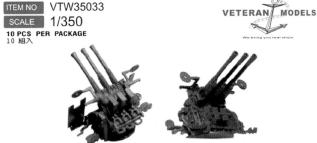

VETERAN MODELS

WHITE ENSIGN MODELS
1/350 scale

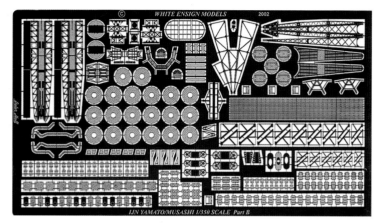

White Ensign Models (WEM) of the United Kingdom is a company that has been in the after-market photo-etch business for some time now and has built a fine reputation based on good research, the very high quality of its products, and the extent and range of its output. For the *Yamato* class battleships WEM has produced a very fine set of photo-etch in 1/350 scale. Both sheets of brass etch are pictured here, and as can be seen the sets are quite comprehensive. WEM also offers an extensive line of naval paints in historically correct shades, as well as a painting guide to the IJN.

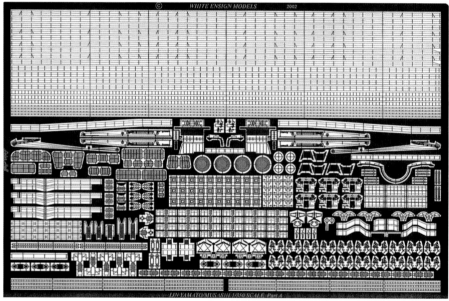

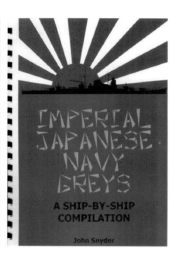

SHINSENGUMI
1/350 scale

This is a real wood replacement deck, to scale, for the Tamiya 1/350 *Yamato* class battleship plastic kits, produced by Shinsengumi of Japan, and available through Hobby Link Japan (HLJ). This relatively new company started by manufacturing real wood decks for plastic ship model kits, initially for IJN subjects, but they have recently released wood deck kits for warships of other navies of the Second World War period. These real wood decks are laser scribed and produced in sheets of incredibly thin veneer. Any model builder using them will need to cut the fittings off the kit's plastic deck and re-position them on this new wood deck, but the end result is nothing short of spectacular, and well worth the trouble. Very highly recommended, but only for the advanced kit assembler. Real wood decks for other ships are available in 1/700, 1/350 and 1/200 scales. Note that Shinsengumi also produces brass gun barrels and decals for wood decking.

Modelmakers' Showcase

The models on display in this section of the book depict both the *Yamato* and the *Musashi* at various times during their short careers. They represent some of the best examples from around the world, constructed by advanced kit builders, or highly proficient scratch builders. All the models which began life as kits feature many of the after-market products surveyed in this publication, and most, including those scratch-built, will have used the reference material also presented here.

This section is usually confined to the work of hobbyists, but in this volume we include two spectacular and unusual 'models', the first a huge 1/10 scale professionally-made exhibit at the Kure Naval Museum, and the other a full-size film set of *Yamato*. Both provide an outstanding degree of detailed reference.

Tamiya 1/350 *Yamato*.

Tamiya 1/700 *Musashi*.

Full-size 'Men of the *Yamato*' movie set.

TAMIYA *MUSASHI* 1/700 scale   by L MOSBEAK

Musashi built by Lars Juel Mosbeak of Germany from the newest tooling from Tamiya Plastic Model Co of Japan. As can be seen in the images of this model, extensive additions of photo-etch details were made. The photo-etch sets used were from Tom's Modelworks, Eduard, Voyager and Lion Roar. The wood decking was reproduced by using the kit deck and painting it with three colours of paint, in layers of washes and individual thin strokes until the desired look was achieved. Many details were scratch-built, using all of the reference books listed in this publication. *Musashi* is depicted as she appeared in July 1943.

This view of *Musashi* is a wonderful evocation of how she would have appeared at anchor off Truk in 1943.

The photo below illustrates the configuration of *Musashi* at that period in her career.

Musashi had the pair of 25mm triple AA mounts added on the main deck, both port and starboard, soon after her commissioning.

The photos to the left and below illustrates the layout of aircraft-handling facilities aboard *Musashi*. All of the aircraft on this model are Mitsubishi F1M floatplanes (Allied code name 'Pete'), which were used for reconnaissance purposes.

TAMIYA *YAMATO* 1/350 scale

by P VAN BUREN

This model of *Yamato*, built by Peter Van Buren of the United States, was constructed from the Tamiya kit that has been available since the early 1980s. The level of detail in the construction on this model is very high, achieved by Mr Van Buren using two sets of photo-etch, from Gold Medal Models and Lion Roar.

This model also benefited from the use of the wood deck kit from Shinsengumi, which

makes a huge contribution to the overall look of realism. Note the rope reels at the breakwater, where sewing thread was used to make them look as natural as possible.

The rigging of this model kit was done with the smallest fishing line available, and included the lines associated with handling boats and aircraft – just one example of the

extra efforts made by Mr Van Buren to replicate exactly the features of the real ship.

The construction and precise painting of the ship's aircraft made them miniature model kits in their own right. Probably unique to this build of the 1/350 Tamiya kit is the rigging of the aircraft off the stern of *Yamato*; this author has never seen this attempted before on any built-up model of the *Yamato* class. The weathering of this model is also very well done, and contributes much to the overall impression.

TAMIYA *MUSASHI* 1/350 scale

by Y LEE

Musashi, built by Young-ho Lee, was constructed from the Tamiya kit that, like that of its sister-ship, has been available since the early 1980s. This is a very clean build of this warship in her October 1944 configuration at the Battle of Leyte Gulf.

Mr Lee's build of *Musashi* used the Lion Roar photo-etch set. The painting of the kit's plastic deck was very well done, giving it a realistic look that is difficult to obtain. The rigging is very delicate and also very realistic in both its scale and effect. The painting of the model kit is clean and correct with just the right amount of weathering not to distract from the quality of this build-up.

YAMATO 1/1 SCALE   MOVIE SET

In December 2005 a movie called *Otoko-tachi Yamato* ('Men of the *Yamato*') opened in Japan. It is a story of life aboard the super-battleship from a crewman's perspective at the time of her last voyage. To make this movie, a full-size set of the *Yamato* was constructed. These are photos of that set, taken by Hideharu Murai of Osaka, Japan.

Unfortunately, the upper bridge, funnel and mainmast could not be built due to building code restrictions, but the first impression is still the massive size of this ship.

Because of the accuracy and realism of this set's construction, roaming its deck must have brought back memories for IJN veterans. All of these photos were taken after the filming of the movie was over, when the set was open to the public. The portion of the warship that is 'missing', was superimposed by using footage taken of Kure Museum's 1/10 scale *Yamato* model.

One can see the evidence of filming the *Yamato*'s final battle in the blackened and burnt areas, as well as paint chipping. The set was constructed mostly of wood atop a steel framework. Many of the details were resin castings. The image below was taken while the movie was being filmed; the amount of pyrotechnics that were expended during that sequence is obvious. The fine details built into this set can be seen in the makeup of the triple 25mm AA mount in the photo to the right. This model, or set, has now been dismantled and no longer exists.

NICHIMO *YAMATO* 1/200 scale

by H OHANIAN

This model of *Yamato*, built by Harry Ohanian of the United States, was constructed from the Nichimo kit that has been available since the late 1970s. However, the details of this model form one of the most, if not *the* most, extensive modifications to this kit that has ever been undertaken. For example, the entire wood deck was hand-laid with individual strips of boxwood. Anyone familiar with this kit can clearly see the extent of the corrections and modifications by examining these photos. Mr Ohanian consulted directly with Japan's

leading authority on *Yamato*, Mr K Hara, about the details of this model.

Many of the fine details were derived from the available Gold Medal Models (GMM) photo-etch set, but many more were scratch-built. This was done with brass rod or fine copper wire. The rigging of this model is one of its most impressive features. Many model ships are rigged too heavily, but this model has the rigging as close to scale as possible. This was made with .002 nylon line and .001 linen, both coloured black. The radar antenna are modified GMM photo-etch parts with scratch-built dipoles added. Many other types of antenna were made from scratch.

The aircraft aboard this model of *Yamato* are each a model unto themselves. They

were each re-cast in resin, cockpits hollowed out, detailed and fitted with vacuum-formed canopies. The painting of the aircraft was researched in depth so as to correctly replicate their configuration.

The hull was plated and portholes covered by Mr Ohanian, who also scratch-built all of the details on the funnel. The kit comes in the 1944 'Leyte Gulf' configuration, but was converted to her April 1945 appearance. Altogether, Mr Ohanian spent over 3500 hours in a little more than a three-year long period to construct this magnificent recreation of *Yamato*.

PROFESSIONALLY BUILT *YAMATO* 1/10 scale   by KURE MUSEUM

Yamato, built by the Yamamoto Shipyard Co, Ltd, assisted by the IJN Model Ships Preserving Association and organised by the city of Kure. This massive model was constructed over eight years and was completed in February 2005. The cost was over 200 million Yen, most donated by a single individual. At this scale, the model measures out at a staggering length of just over 86 feet, and forms an astounding main attraction at the Kure City Naval History and Science Museum.

The level of detail in this model is second to none: at this scale, the details have to be

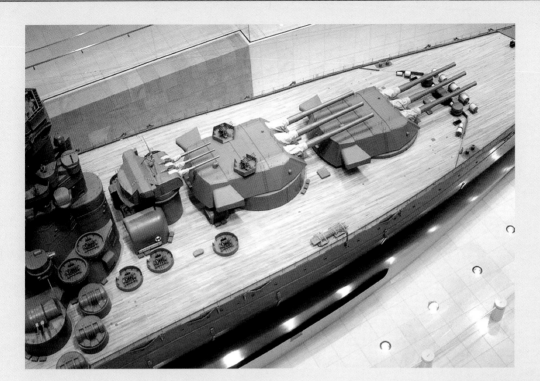

correct, or mistakes will stand out. At the time all of the latest information about this ship was incorporated into the construction of the model, but even in the short space of time since, new details have come to light, making some items incorrect. A list of these can be obtained in a new book about this model, *1/10 Scale Yamato*, from Model Art Publishing, but be sure to ask for the English translation pamphlet to be included. The information about the structure and details to be gleaned by viewing this model are without equal, since even original photographs of the ship only survive in small numbers.

The true size and scale of this model can be appreciated in the photographs showing people in the background. At 1/10 scale, a

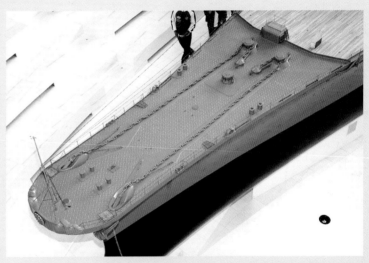

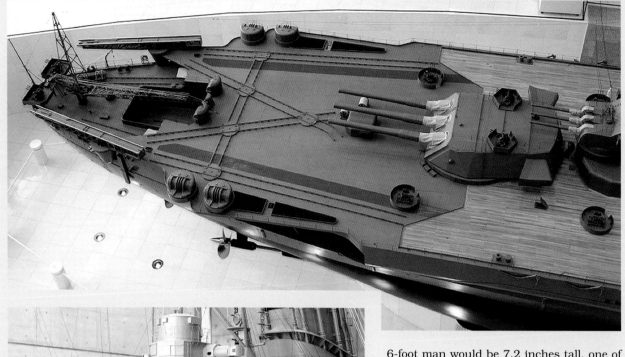

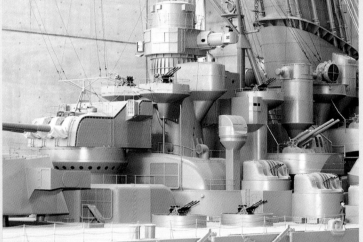

6-foot man would be 7.2 inches tall, one of which is visible on the far right edge of the centre photo on this page. One of the noticeable items missing from this model are the observation aircraft that *Yamato* carried. Although at least one model of a Mitsubishi F1M 'Pete' was constructed, it was not fitted to the model as exhibited. The decking, especially the wood, was very well constructed. Even in photography, this is the most impressive ship model, but for a ship-modelling enthusiast to view it in person must be a unique experience – almost worth the air fare to Japan.

Yamato under construction, during her final fitting-out phase, 20 September 1941. This is a digitally coloured black and white image.

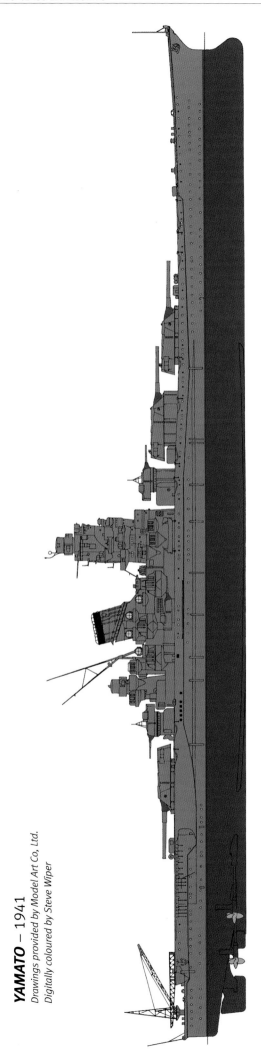

YAMATO – 1941
Drawings provided by Model Art Co, Ltd.
Digitally coloured by Steve Wiper

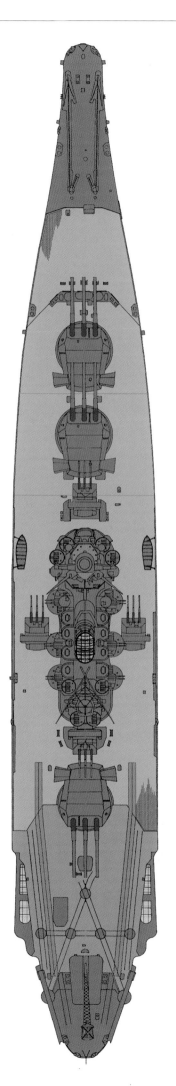

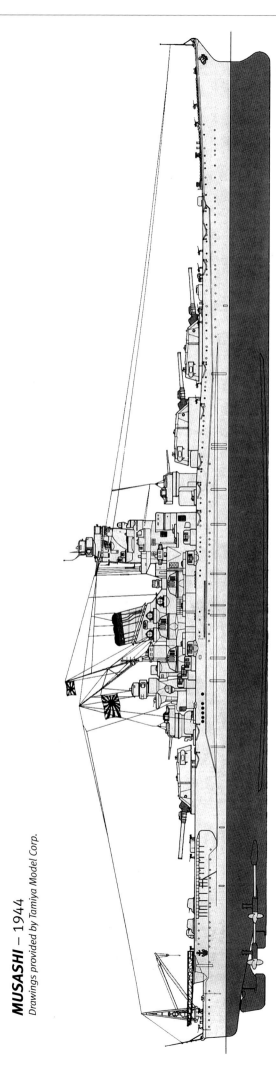

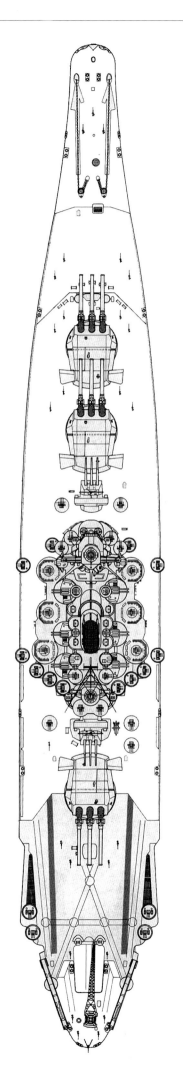

MUSASHI – 1944
Drawings provided by Tamiya Model Corp.

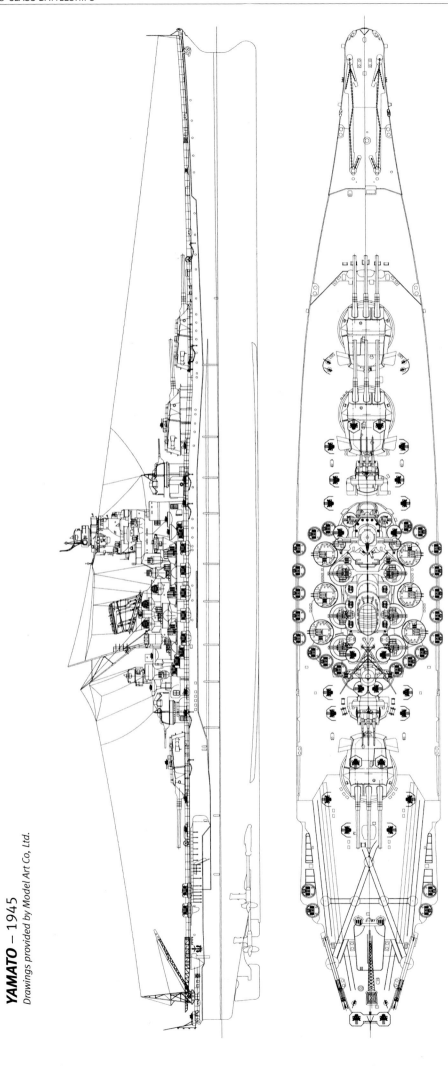

YAMATO – 1945
Drawings provided by Model Art Co, Ltd.

THE FINAL OPERATIONS

The massive four-day engagement that is known as the Battle of Leyte Gulf was actually made up of a number of actions that took place within this time frame. The first of these was a small but disastrous engagement for the Japanese Navy usually called the Battle of the Palawan Passage. Under the leadership of Vice Admiral Kurita, Force A, comprising the battleships *Yamato* (with Admiral Ugaki aboard), *Musashi*, *Nagato*, *Kongo*, *Haruna*, with cruisers and destroyers, left Brunei Bay and steamed north by north-east along the coast of the island of Palawan, north of Borneo. *En route* Force A was ambushed by two American fleet submarines, *Darter* and *Dace*. At 5:30am on 23 October 1944 each submarine fired a spread of six torpedoes at the oncoming Japanese task force. Vice Admiral Kurita's flagship was the heavy cruiser *Atago*, which along with her sister-

ship *Maya* were sunk, while another sister-ship, the *Takao*, was severely damaged, but managed to limp back to Singapore. Losing three major combatants before engaging the enemy fleet was a serious blow to the IJN, but Vice Admiral Kurita was rescued from the sea by a destroyer and later transferred to the battleship *Yamato*. The two American submarines waited until nightfall and attempted to move in for the kill on the damaged *Takao*, but suddenly *Darter* ran hard aground and became a total loss, although her crew were later rescued by *Dace*, providing for the Americans a satisfactory conclusion to the Battle of the Palawan Passage.

Force A re-grouped and through the night Vice Admiral Kurita's reduced but still powerful task force continued on their course towards the Philippine Islands. In the early hours of the morning Force A was headed in a easterly direction, rounding the southern end of the island of Mindoro and

Below: Not the best quality image, but one of very few of the aircraft handling facilities aboard the *Yamato* class. The aircraft in this photograph is a Mitsubishi F1M2 floatplane, Allied code name 'Pete'. This photo was taken aboard the *Musashi* about May 1944. The cylindrical object to the left of aircraft crane boom support is one of two machine gun directors fitted during the major AA upgrade both warships received. The squared-off blast shielding on that director identifies the ship as *Musashi*.

Musashi steaming out of Brunei Bay, as part of Force A, 22 October 1944, *en route* to attack American forces landing at Leyte.

proceeding through the Tablas Strait. The new day brought a new battle: at 8:10am on 24 October *Yamato* spotted three American scout planes at 31 miles distant, shadowing Force A. *Musashi* was busy for over an hour trying to jam the scout planes' radio transmissions, but obviously to no avail.

By 10:18am a wave of at least 45 American aircraft was sighted, and at 10:26am Force A opened fire on the approaching aircraft, thus beginning the Battle of the Sibuyan Sea. By 10:45am this first attack was over, the American aircraft having concentrated their attentions on *Musashi*. Several near miss bombs cause minor leaking in her bow, while another hit atop turret No 1, but with no effect. A torpedo, however, hit *Musashi* on her starboard side amidships, causing major flooding. The shock from the blast of that torpedo hit also jammed *Musashi*'s main director. Counter-flooding corrected the list and the super-battleship steamed on with about 3000 tons of water and a 1-degree list to starboard. After a brief lull, at 11:54am Force A detected more aircraft approaching.

By 12:45pm the next wave of American carrier-based aircraft attacked Force A, concentrating upon the capital ships. This group of aircraft was of the same strength as the last, and the mixture of dive and torpedo bombers scored two bomb hits, five near misses and three torpedo hits amidships on the port side on *Musashi*, as well as two bomb hits on *Yamato*. *Yamato* was able to maintain speed and her fighting

capability, but *Musashi*, with severe damage to the AA gun mounts and crews and down six feet by the bow, was slowed to 22 knots. Both of the super-battleships were firing their shotgun-like AA shells at the attacking aircraft from their main armament during these engagements. Aboard *Musashi*, as one such shell was being loaded into the breech, a bomb fragment somehow found its was down the muzzle of the centre gun of the No 1 main turret and caused the 18.1in AA ammunition to ignite, destroying the interior of the turret and rendering it inoperable. Just as this wave of attacking aircraft departed, another swooped in for a further attack.

At 1:30pm 24 carrier aircraft attacked, again concentrating upon *Musashi*, then showing visible signs of distress. Although Force A slowed to help *Musashi* keep up and protect her with the fleet's AA fire, *Musashi* received damage from strafing by American fighter aircraft, two bomb hits abreast the No 3 main turret, four bomb hits abreast Nos 1 and 2 main gun turrets, and four torpedo hits on the hull. The first torpedo hit was starboard amidships, the second was on the starboard bow, the third portside abreast No 1 main gun turret and the fourth was portside amidships. *Musashi* was then down 13 feet by the bow with speed reduced to 19 knots. *Yamato* received only minor damage during this attack, but once again, it was followed almost immediately by another, this one aimed at *Yamato* and *Nagato*.

Force A scattered when American aircraft began their attack in the Sibuyan Sea. *Yamato* is the large warship to the left displaying an impressively tight turning circle, while the *Musashi* is the vessel obscured by smoke, already taking hits from the dive bombers.

Death of the *Musashi*
This sequence of photographs illustrates the attack by American carrier-based dive and torpedo bombers on the *Musashi* in the Sibuyan Sea, 24 October 1944. In these images, one can see how the bombers overwhelmed the IJN task force, but concentrated on *Musashi*.

The bottom image is of the *Musashi* limping towards an island in an attempt to beach herself, which she failed to do and sank within sight of land. Note how the stem-head is above water, but the forecastle between the stem and the No 1 main gun turret is awash.

Both of the photographs above are of *Yamato* taking a bomb hit on, or just forward of, the No 1 main gun turret. These images were taken during the American attack upon Force A during the Battle of the Sibuyan Sea, 24 October 1944.

At this time, 2:15pm, Vice Admiral Kurita ordered Force A to increase speed to 22 knots, leaving *Musashi* behind. During this fourth attack by American carrier aircraft, *Yamato* was hit by five bombs, causing major damage and giving the ship a 5-degree list to port. Counter-flooding and damage control reduce the list to less than 1 degree, but she was down at the bow by 2 feet. *Nagato* received two bomb hits, temporarily slowing her to 20 knots, but she managed repairs and was able to return to the fleet speed of 22 knots. The heavy cruiser *Myoko* was also hit by a torpedo in the stern and disabled. She would later limp back to Singapore. This attack was over by 2:45pm.

In the meantime *Musashi* slowed to 8 knots and had dropped far behind Force A, the effects of the serious damage from the numerous attacks escalating all the time. Again, at 2:55pm, yet another wave of American carrier aircraft pounced on the crippled battleship. A force of 69 aircraft pounded the super-battleship in this fifth attack upon Force A. *Musashi* received four bomb and three more torpedo hits, and numerous near misses during this assault. As the American aircraft left the scene, they reported that the super-battleship was trailing oil, on fire, wreathed in heavy smoke, and dead in the water. Damage to *Musashi* is difficult to determine at this

Yamato manoeuvring wildly in an attempt to avoid USN destroyer-launched torpedoes during the Battle off Samar. The battleship in the background is either the *Kongo* or *Haruna*.

point. She had received hit after hit, and the number of dead, especially amongst her AA crews, must have been staggering. Nonetheless, her damage control teams – or what was left of them – were able to counter-flood and somewhat control her list. They were able to get the vessel moving once again at 8 knots, although by this stage her bow was almost under water.

But there was no respite: a sixth attack by American aircraft began almost as the previous wave flew off. It seemed like whole wings of US Navy aircraft were circling, waiting for their turn at the struggling giant. The American air crews were amazed that any battleship could withstand this level of punishment, but they pressed home their attacks regardless. The next round began at 3:45pm with another combined dive and torpedo bomber attack, aimed at the *Musashi* alone. She was hit with ten bombs during this phase, decimating what was left of the AA gun crews. One bomb hit the bridge, killing over 50 crew; another penetrated to the boiler rooms, knocking out two of them. Also during this attack *Musashi* was struck by as many as nine torpedoes, hitting her on both the port and starboard sides, some in the vicinity of previous hits, the explosions digging deeper into the already ravaged hull. As the last of the American aircraft departed the area at about 4:20pm, they observed a burning, smoking wreck of what used to be one of the most powerful battleships ever constructed, dead in the water, listing at least 9 degrees, with a couple of destroyers moving in to lend assistance.

Musashi took on an 11-degree list to port, but this was partially corrected by counter-flooding, although only for a short time. The flooding by this stage was uncontrollable and progressing at a steady rate. She was able to get underway, at about 5 knots, but soon even this would not be possible. Force A reversed course about 4:30pm and was headed back towards *Musashi*, but Vice Admiral Kurita soon realized that her situation was hopeless and resumed his original course eastward

towards the island of Samar, although he did instruct the heavy cruiser *Tone* and destroyers to remain with *Musashi* and lend what assistance they could. The captain of the doomed battleship was then attempting to head north towards the Bondoc Peninsula to beach the ship. The port anchor was let go, anything not bolted down was jettisoned, and even the crew were moved to the starboard side aft, in an attempt to counter the list. Crawling along at 4 to 5 knots, the bow down 26 feet, forecastle awash, the engines finally gave out and she slowed to a stop, still burning in the area of the superstructure. At 7:15pm, when *Musashi*'s list had increased to 12 degrees to port, the captain gave the order to prepare to abandon ship and for the crew to assemble aft. By 7:30pm, with most of the crew drawn up on the aircraft deck, her list having then reached 30 degrees to port, the captain finally gave the order to abandon ship. *Musashi* slowly rolled over to port and capsized at 7:36pm, at location 13°07' North by 122°32' East, about 2.5 miles south-west of Bondoc Point. Three destroyers rescued about 1379 crew, plus 635 survivors from the heavy cruiser *Maya*, sunk the day before. Including those lost when the ship went down, casualties totalled about 1023 of the crew.

The *Yamato* and the heavy cruiser *Tone* running at high speed during their attack on the US escort carriers in the Battle off Samar.

The *Yamato* taking high-speed avoiding action in the Tablas Strait when the retreating Force A was attacked by USAAF B-24 bombers on 26 October 1944.

Japanese sources indicate that *Musashi* was hit by eleven torpedoes and ten bombs, while American records stated that they hit her with twenty torpedoes and seventeen bombs, plus fifteen near misses. In either case, this was a massive amount of punishment that no warship could survive. Approximately 260 US Navy aircraft attacked the IJN surface fleet in this 6-hour running battle across the Sibuyan Sea, during which the Japanese were only able to shoot down 18 American aircraft.

The remains of Force A, with battleships

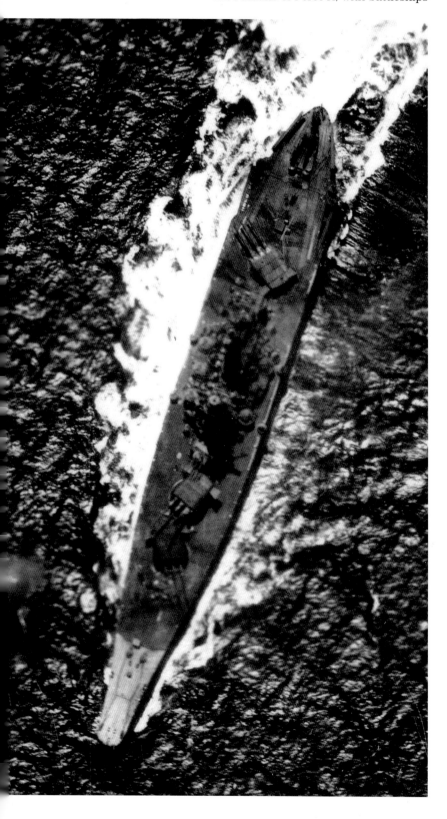

Yamato, *Nagato*, *Kongo* and *Haruna*, cruisers and destroyers proceeded out of the Sibuyan Sea that night, towards the open ocean and the Philippine Sea. *Yamato* had sustained three bomb hits, but they caused minimal damage. At the time of the sinking of *Musashi*, Force A was midway down the west coast of the island of Burias, and by 9:00pm they were rounding the northern tip of the island of Ticao and headed south towards the entrance of the San Bernardino Strait. Force A passed through that strait in single file at about midnight.

Yamato, Vice Admiral Kurita's flagship, then entered the Philippine Sea in the early hours, of 25 October 1944, steaming in a easterly direction. Force A changed course to the south, along the eastern coast of the island of Samar, towards Leyte Gulf and the American invasion force landing there. Kurita's intention was to attack the American amphibious shipping with his battleships and cruisers.

At 5:23am *Yamato*'s radar picked up ships further to the south, in the path of Force A's advance, near the south-eastern end of the island of Samar. By 5:45am Force A sighted ships on the horizon, identified them as six small aircraft carriers, with cruisers and destroyers. *Yamato* immediately opened fire on these ships, but the remainder of Force A was not able to open fire until they were within range (which was at 5:58am). This was the beginning of what was to be called the Battle off Samar. The actual task force under attack by Force A was six escort carriers, three destroyers and four destroyer escorts, and as *Yamato* and Force A fired at the American carriers, the US Navy destroyers and DEs put up a smoke screen to help defend their carriers. *Yamato* launched some of her observation aircraft to help spot her fire upon the US carriers, and about the same time aircraft from the US escort carriers, armed with whatever weapons were to hand, made diversionary attacks on Force A.

About 6:55am American destroyers charged out of the smoke screen towards the Japanese force, launching a torpedo attack. The Japanese battleships concentrated their fire on the threat posed by the American destroyers, while the Japanese cruisers continued to fire at the carriers. The US torpedo attack was partially successful, even though the only hit obtained was on the heavy cruiser *Kumano*, putting her out of action and forcing her to retire towards the San Bernardino Strait. However, torpedo wakes were spotted by the battleships, causing them to scatter, with *Yamato* and *Nagato* turning north in an attempt to outrun them, putting them out of the battle area. *Kongo* and *Haruna* remained, but were kept busy dodging torpedo wakes and attacking aircraft. At 7:30am the IJN heavy cruiser *Suzuya* was hit and disabled by near misses from

bombs. Meanwhile, the American escort carriers were able to hide in rain squalls in their area.

The rain squalls came to an end about 8:00am and the Japanese assault on the USN carriers and escorts recommenced. The IJN heavy cruiser *Haguro* led *Chokai*, *Chikuma* and *Tone* south in an attempt to catch the American escort carriers, while *Yamato*, *Nagato*, *Kongo* and *Haruna* battled the escorting destroyers. *Yamato* fired on a charging US destroyer, which disappeared in a cloud of smoke, and *Kongo* dealt likewise with another destroyer. The battleships then turned their attention to the escort carriers but, of hundreds of rounds expended, only a few hits were obtained. In this one-sided running battle between Japanese big-gun surface ships and the American escort carriers and destroyers, the Americans managed to fend off near-certain annihilation by the sacrifice of the destroyers, which attacked with torpedoes several times, causing the Japanese battle force to scatter and giving the carriers time to escape. The Japanese battleships and cruisers were able to sink only three American destroyers and one escort carrier. The Americans did have the advantage of carrier aircraft to attack the Japanese force, and these caused significant losses, sinking the heavy cruisers *Suzuya*, *Chokai* and *Chikuma*. Vice Admiral Kurita ordered Force A to reverse course several times, which enabled the American escort carriers to escape to the south towards Leyte Gulf.

At about 12:30pm American carrier aircraft attacked Force A, which turned north to evade them and retreat. *Yamato* was undamaged in that engagement, but *Nagato* was hit by one bomb on the foredeck (with minor damage), *Kongo* was damaged by several near misses, but *Haruna* was unscathed. At 4:55pm, Force A was again attacked by US carrier aircraft, but not damaged.

About 9:00pm on 25 October 1944 Vice Admiral Kurita's fleet, lead by *Yamato*, entered the San Bernardino Strait, headed west. All that remained of the once powerful Force A were the battleships *Yamato*, *Nagato*, *Kongo* and *Haruna*, the heavy cruisers *Haguro* and *Tone*, and destroyers. During the night, Force A was joined by the badly damaged heavy cruisers *Kumano* and *Myoko* as they limped westward, back through the Sibuyan Sea.

Dawn on 26 October 1944 found Kurita headed south through the Tablas Strait, east of the island of Mindoro. At about 8:00am the exhausted Japanese task force was attacked by US Navy carrier aircraft for about one hour. *Yamato* was hit by two bombs with only minor damage, but the light cruiser *Noshiro* was sunk. Several other warships were slightly damaged by near misses, but they managed to regroup and continue south. At 10:40am, approximately 30 USAAF B-24 bombers made a high-level attack. No direct hits were scored, but there was damage to *Haruna* from several near misses. On 27 October in

Both the photograph on this and the previous page are of *Yamato* manoeuvring to evade the fall of bombs from B-24 bombers. The American aerial photography from this attack is some of the best that has survived of the *Yamato*. The ship does not seem to be putting up much AA fire, but she was not hit during this attack, although there were several near misses.

The officers of *Yamato*, taken on 5 April 1945, the day before departing on their final mission. An interesting detail is the inside face of the watertight door to the right edge of this image.

the Palawan Passage the battleships refuelled several destroyers running low on fuel. Also on that day, Force A buried their dead at sea (29 on *Yamato*), and following day arrived back at Brunei Bay.

Yamato and the other warships refuelled upon their arrival, but were unable to replenish their ammunition until 6 November, when a carrier and light cruiser arrived from Japan carrying those supplies. During that time minor repairs were carried out aboard *Yamato* and the other warships present. On 8 November the battleships *Yamato*, *Nagato*, *Kongo* and *Haruna* put to sea for four days to avoid air attacks on Brunei Bay. Battleship Division One was disbanded on the 15th and *Yamato* became flagship of the IJN Second Fleet.

On 16 November *Yamato*, in company with *Nagato*, *Kongo*, the light cruiser *Yahagi* and destroyers, sailed from Brunei Bay for Japan, but *en route* the task force was

ambushed by the American submarine *Sealion*. At 3:00am on 21 November, in the Formosa Strait, the American submarine fired first the six bow tubes, and after turning, the four stern tubes at the IJN task force. Three or four torpedoes struck *Kongo* and one hit a destroyer, which sank immediately. *Kongo* sheered out of line and took on a severe list; she eventually sank at about 5:30am, just north of Formosa. *Yamato* and the rest of the task force safely reached Japan, entering the Kure Navy Yard on 23 November 1944.

Yamato went into the dry dock at the yard two days later for a very much needed repair and refit. Bomb damage to her superstructure and fore deck was repaired and all but two of the single 25mm AA mounts were removed and replaced with nine triple 25mm AA mounts, giving her a final outfit of 152 of these light AA guns. On 23 December Vice Admiral Ito would assume

Taken from an American Helldiver dive bomber as it pulled up from its attack on the *Yamato*, this photo shows the additional triple 25mm enclosed AA mounts at the deck edge amidships. At the time of this photo *Yamato* had taken a few hits to the centre of the superstructure.

In this image, taken by the same aircraft that snapped the photo on the previous page, one can see that the bomb missed its mark by a wide margin, causing no damage to the *Yamato*.

command of the Second Fleet and on 1 January 1945 *Yamato*, *Nagato* and *Haruna* were assigned to the reactivated Battleship Division One, Second Fleet. By 3 January *Yamato* had been undocked and the repairs and refit were complete by 15 January. She departed Kure for Hashirajima Anchoring Area, located 30–40km south of the naval base at Kure.

On 10 February 1945 BatDiv 1 and the Second Fleet were disbanded and *Yamato* was assigned to Carrier Division 1. Perhaps indicative of the nervous state of the ship's crew, on 13 March while still sitting at the Hashirajima Anchorage, *Yamato* accidentally fired on Japanese aircraft overhead. Four days later she returned to Kure Navy Yard and on the 19th a massive air raid by US Navy carrier aircraft was launched against the yard and the warships in Kure Bay. *Yamato* steamed out to the Inland Sea and was hit by one small bomb on her superstructure. On 28 March the majority of the fleet, including *Yamato*, was ordered to Sasebo Navy Yard on the north-western coast of Kyushu, but was recalled the same day as US Navy carrier aircraft raided southern Kyushu. At this point the Imperial Japanese Navy planned to anchor its remaining warships in remote locations to make it more difficult for the Americans to find them.

On 3 April 1945 Admiral Ito received new orders: *Yamato*, the light cruiser *Yahagi* and eight destroyers were to undertake a 'Kamikaze' mission against the American invasion forces attacking Okinawa, a mere 400 miles to the south-west of Kyushu. The next day was spent on AA gunnery practice, and on the 5th a detailed planning meeting took place aboard *Yamato* for her final mission as flagship of the Surface Special Attack Unit. This mission was named 'Ten-Ichi-Go', which translated literally meant 'Heaven Number One.' The mission was to steam undetected to the north-west of Okinawa and make a high speed run in on the American invasion forces and destroy as many enemy vessels as possible. At that time, the task force was topped up with almost all the remaining fuel oil the IJN could muster – but not enough for a round trip.

On 6 April 1945 *Yamato* and the other warships of the Surface Special Attack Unit departed for their final mission, sailing at 3:30pm. The Japanese task force was spotted by the American submarine *Threadfin* at about 9:30pm, which reported the sighting to the US Navy forward head-

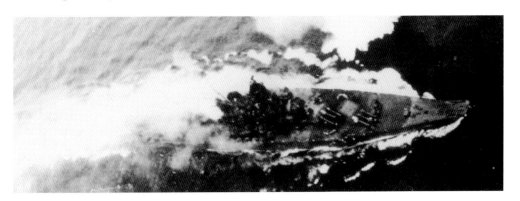

This photo of *Yamato* was taken at 1:35pm, 7 April 1945, a short time after the two previous photographs.

All of the photographs on this and following pages are a sequence of images of the final battle of the *Yamato*. In this image, *Yamato* (right) has just been hit by a bomb while the light cruiser *Yahagi* is still manoeuvring to avoid the attacking US Navy carrier-based aircraft.

Right: *Yamato* has just taken a torpedo hit to the port bow, throwing up a huge cascade of water. Her escorting destroyers are also fighting for their lives against an overwhelming number of American aircraft.

Below: *Yamato* turning hard to port, but her speed is down considerably at this point. There is a fire raging at her after superstructure.

quarters on Guam. During the night *Yamato* and the task force passed the southern end of Kyushu and headed west into the East China Sea. The Japanese task force had some air cover, based on Kyushu, but it was sporadic at best. About 8:30am on the 7th the IJN task force was spotted by an American search aircraft from the carrier *Essex*, and later by more American aircraft. By 11:30am small groups of aircraft had gathered and were circling above IJN task force, waiting for more to join.

The attack upon *Yamato* and her task force finally began at around 12:30pm and lasted about twenty minutes. This first wave comprised 280 aircraft from nine US Navy aircraft carriers, and almost immediatel, a destroyer was sunk, while *Yamato*'s bridge was strafed. She was then hit by two bombs, amidships and on the aftermost secondary 6in turret. *Yamato* was hit by two more bombs in the same vicinity, causing severe damage to her after superstructure and the 6in magazine, and producing a

fierce fire in this area. Torpedoes began to strike the ship from port – a lesson learned by the Americans in their attack upon her sister-ship *Musashi* was that the massive breadth of the *Yamato* class battleships required all torpedo hits to be on one side only; hits on the other side merely saved the Japanese crew the task of counter-flooding. In this first wave of attacks *Yamato* took four torpedo hits on the port side, causing about 3000 tons of flooding, initially resulting a 6-degree list, but soon corrected to about 1 or 2 degrees. At the same time strafing of the superstructure by fighter aircraft also reduced the number of operational 25mm mounts. During this first wave of attacks, the light cruiser *Yahagi* was hit by one torpedo and went dead in the water.

The second phase began at 1:00pm, and during this attack American bombers launched their torpedoes from many directions, ensuring multiple hits. *Yamato* was hit by three or four torpedoes to port and one to starboard. The portside hits caused

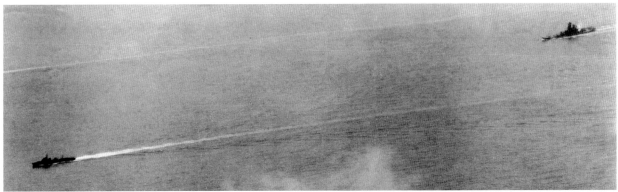

the ship to take on a severe list of 15 to 18 degrees, but the starboard hit in effect produced counter-flooding that reduced the list to 10 degrees. *Yamato* was in a very poor state by that time, because with a list at 10 degrees or more she could not use her main batteries, which fired special 'shotgun' AA rounds, against the swarms of American aircraft. There were several bomb hits, decimating more of the AA gun crews stationed in the open mounts, highlighting one of the shortcomings of the *Yamato* class design – the AA mounts were grouped so closely together that one large bomb hit knocked out several at a time.

Within 5 or 10 minutes of the second attack ending, at 1:45pm the third wave of US Navy aircraft descended upon the *Yamato* and the IJN task force. This time *Yamato* was hit by three large bombs amidships, which blew holes in her main deck and even blasted several of the shielded deck-edge 25mm AA mounts right off the ship and into the ocean. Another bomb hit the foredeck, severing the port anchor chain, with the 15-ton main anchor and chain sinking to the bottom of the sea. There were

also numerous near misses that sprang leaks in the hull plating and caused significant interior damage due to concussion. *Yamato* was hit by four torpedoes during this attack that sealed her fate. Three of them were on the port side, with the fourth on the starboard side. Many of the firerooms and machinery spaces were holed and flooded, reducing *Yamato*'s speed to a mere 10 knots, running on one shaft. Both the main and the auxiliary rudders were out of action and in a hard-over position to port. She was on fire in the area of the after superstructure and smoking heavily, steaming in a large slow circle, out of control.

In the meantime, the other warships of the IJN Surface Special Attack Unit were taking a beating. The light cruiser *Yahagi* was already dead in the water from a torpedo hit in the first wave, but was hit by a total of twelve bombs and six additional torpedoes by the end of the third wave of attacks. *Yahagi* sank rapidly at 2:05pm on 7 April 1945, in position 30°40' North by 128°03' East. By the end of the attacks, four of the original eight destroyers in the Surface Special Attack Unit had also been sunk. The

Above: *Yamato* is now down noticeably by the bow from successive torpedo hits. Smoke from a fire in her after superstructure can still be seen. An escorting destroyer is making a high speed run on the left of this image.

Below: Just as this photograph was taken, the after guns of an *Akizuki* class destroyer fired – possibly at the aircraft carrying the camera. *Yamato* is smoking from bomb hits and down at the bow from multiple torpedo hits. Her speed is about 15 knots due to other torpedo hits amidships.

In this blurred and grainy photograph, *Yamato* can be seen to be heavily down at the bow and listing at least 10 degrees. The fire in her after superstructure is now out of control.

Destruction of the *Yamato*

The sequence of photographs on this page dramatically depict the end of the super-battleship *Yamato*. After a well coordinated attack by American carrier aircraft, the once-mighty warship began to capsize, then exploded in the most sensational fashion. Reportedly, this explosion was seen as far as 125 miles away.

The top image was taken at the moment of the colossal explosion of the forward magazine.

Below: An measure of the size of the explosion is the 388ft long destroyer in the foreground.

Below, right: A huge mushroom cloud billows up, as the *Yamato* is blown in two and scattered across the sea floor.

first, *Asashimo* at position 31°00' North by 128°00' East, with *Hamakaze* and *Isokaze* together at position 30°40' North by 128°03' East, very near to the light cruiser *Yahagi*. The destroyer *Kasumi* was sunk at 30°57' North by 127°57' East. The survivors, the damaged destroyers *Suzutsuki Hatsushimo*, *Yukikaze*, and *Fuyuzuki*, all managed to rescue survivors and return to Japan.

The *Yamato*, however, was doomed, and the end was near. At about 2:15pm the after magazine temperature warning lights were flashing on the bridge, but that magazine could not be flooded because of the complete loss of power in the battleship by 2:20pm. The list was so severe by then that loose objects and damaged AA gun mounts began to topple into the sea. At 2:23pm *Yamato* rapidly capsized to port, so much so that many crewmen were still below decks, as there was not an 'abandon ship' order given. As the massive and once mighty battleship rolled over to about 120 degrees, her magazines erupted into one of the most massive explosions ever recorded. There was a brilliant flash, followed by a large mushroom cloud of smoke, rising thousands of feet into the air. This was seen as far as 125 miles away. When the smoke cleared, nothing was left. When *Yamato* set out on this last mission, she had a crew of about 3332 men, of whom only 279 were rescued by the four remaining destroyers. Admiral Ito was not among them. She sank at 30°22' North by 128°04' East, in the East China Sea, not half-way to her intended destination.

In total, during all of the attacks over a two-hour period, the *Yamato* was hit by thirteen torpedoes (eleven to port and one to starboard), eight bombs, and numerous near miss bombs that did great shock damage. The destruction was so massive, and the blows so rapid and repetitive, that the damage-control parties had little chance to counter the flooding. In fact, many of these teams were wiped out by the intense pounding *Yamato* was taking. Because of the close proximity of the light AA mounts, grouped tightly around the superstructure, bomb hits and strafing were very effective in knocking them out, quickly eroding the ship's defensive capacity. It was at this time that what was once the third largest navy in the world, steadily decimated throughout the Pacific War, ceased to exist as a viable fighting force. In sharp contrast, the American forces deployed in this attack – approximately 386 carrier-based aircraft of 180 fighters, 75 dive bombers, and 131 torpedo bombers – lost 10 aircraft and 12 air crewmen.

THE WRECK OF THE *YAMATO*

The *Yamato* was sunk at 30°22' North by 128°04' East, in the East China Sea. A Japanese expedition first located the wreck on 1 August 1985, and the wreck was again investigated more thoroughly in 1999. She lies in two main parts in some 1000 feet of water, with a very large debris field surrounding the majority of the wreck.

These are two views of a diorama built for the Tamiya Model Corporation of Japan in 1/350 scale, showing the present appear-ance of the wreck of the *Yamato*, as she lies on the bottom of the East China Sea. As one can see, the damage from the forward maga-zine explosion was very extensive. The after magazine also detonated, producing one of the most extensive debris fields around a wreck ever found in any underwater expedi-tion. The modellers who constructed this diorama are to be commended for their meticulous work, which gives the public a good impression of the present state of the wreck and a clearer idea of what happened to the ship in her final moments.

Additional References

See page 17 for primary references

Campbell, John, *Naval Weapons of World War Two*, Conway Maritime Press (London 1985)

Dulin, R & Garzke, W, *Battleships: Axis & Neutral Battleships in WWII*, Naval Institute Press (Annapolis 1985)

Dull, Paul S, *Battle History of the Imperial Japanese Navy (1941-1945)*, Naval Institute Press (Annapolis 1978)

Francillon, Rene J, *Japanese Aircraft off the Pacific War*, Putnam (London 1987)

Friedman, Norman, *Naval Radar*, Conway Maritime Press (London 1981)

——, *Naval Firepower: Battleship guns and Gunnery in the Dreadnought Era*, Seaforth Publishing (Barnsley 2008)

Gardiner, Robert (ed), *Conway's All The World's Fighting Ships, 1922-1946*, Conway Maritime Press & Naval Institute Press (London & Annapolis 1980)

Government Printing Office, *US Strategic Bombing Survey – Pacific War*, Government Printing Office (Washington, DC 1946)

Mitsuru, Yoshida, *Requiem for Battleship Yamato*, University of Washington Press (Seattle 1985)

Morrison, Samuel Eliot, *History of US Naval Operations in WWII*, Vols 1–15, Little Brown (Boston 1951)

Naval Intelligence, US Division of, *Japanese Naval Vessels of WWII*, ONI 41-42, Naval Institute Press (Annapolis 1987).

Skulski, Janusz, *Anatomy of the Ship: The Battleship Yamato*, Conway Maritime Press & Naval Institute Press (London & Annapolis 1988)

Spurr, Russell, *A Glorious Way To Die*, Newmarket Press (New York 1981)

Wiper, Steve, *Warship Pictorial 25 – IJN Yamato Class Battleships*, Classic Warships Publishing (Tucson 2004).

Yoshimura, Akira, *Build The Musashi*, Kodansha America (New York 1991).

WARSHIP MODELLING WEBSITES – MANUFACTURERS & SUPPLIERS

www.aeronautic.dk
www.alnavco.com
www.chamame29.web.fc2.com
www.classicwarships.com
www.cybermodeler.com
www.eduard.cz
www.fujimimokei.com
www.gakken.co.jp
www.ghqmodels.com
www.goldmm.com
www.hasegawa-model.co.jp
www.hlj.com
www.h3.dion.ne.jp/~mokei/e-home.htm
www.lionroar.net
www.modelart.jp
www.ModelShip.info/Minekaze
www.modelships.info/veteranmodels
www.modelwarships.com
www.navis-neptun.de
www.pacificfront.com
www.scaleshipyard.com
www.soarart.com
www.steelnavy.com
www.tamiya.com
www.tomsmodelworks.com
http://homepage2.nifty.com/vanguard/intro/main2.htm
www.voyagermodel.com
www.warshipmodelsunderway.com
www.whiteensignmodels.com
www.yankeemodelworks.com

WARSHIP RESEARCH WEBSITES

www.combinedfleet.com
www.history.navy.mil

ACKNOWLEDGEMENTS

Technical assistance: Bob Buchanan, Kurt Greiner, Dan Kaplan, Don S Montgomery

Photography: Author's Collection, US National Archives, US Naval Historical Center

Drawings: Author's Collection, Model Art Publications, Tamiya Model Corporation